CUSTOM MADE

Uncover Your Purpose & Light That Shit Up

By: Chantal Heide

Chantal Heide
www.canadasdatingcoach.com

Ordering Information:
Quantity sales. Special discounts are available on quantity purchases by corporations, associations, and others. For details, contact the publisher at the address above.

Printed in Canada
Chantal Heide.

CUSTOM MADE: UNCOVER YOUR PURPOSE AND LIGHT THAT SHIT UP

p. cm.

ISBN 13 – 978-0994980854
ISBN 10 – 0994980854

1. Body Mind and Spirit – General

First Edition
14 13 12 11 10 / 10 9 8 7 6 5 4 3 2 1

Other books by Chantal Heide

Dating 101 – Understanding the Drives, Behaviours, and Emotions Behind Love

Comeback Queen – 7 Steps to Making a Triumphant Return to Dating After Divorce

Fake Love Need Not Apply – The Single Girls Guide To Avoiding Posers Losers Scammers And Predators Online

No More Assholes – Your 7 Step Guide to Saying Goodbye to Guys and Finding The Real Man You're Looking For

After The First Kiss – Making Your First Year Together Ridiculously Awesome

Fix That Shit – A Couples Guide To Getting Past The Sticky Stuff

Say Yes To Goodness – 10 Steps To A Complete And Happy You

For Dennis, and every dream that's come true since

surrendering to Goodness

Contents

Acknowledgements

My first thank you goes to my husband, the man who showed me that there actually is such a thing as soul mates. Somehow we keep getting better and better, and it blows my mind.

Speaking of minds, I've got to give thanks to the stuff inside my head. Somehow that grey glob generates a ton of ideas, and I've got a lot more waiting to come to life. So, thanks, brain, you've been a trip.

Thank you to my parents. I'm not an easy child to accept, but they've done a bang up job and I'm finally giving them a rest.

Thank you to my friends, because without them my life would be unbalanced. Sometimes you've just got to kick back and chillax with people who can vibe right alongside you.

Thank you to the ladies of Zonta. They are helping unleash parts of me I didn't even realize existed, and I'm absolutely loving my development within this fierce, tribal community who don't accept bullshit towards women.

Thank you to my amazing editor Kit Duncan. It would be hard to find someone funnier to go through my work with a fine tooth comb.

And of course, thank you Maggie and Lulu. There isn't a day where your antics and love don't warm my heart. Both are lying on my office floor right now, Maggie spread out right behind me, and Lulu curled up by the office door as they wait for me to wrap up and do something fun like garden, walk, cuddle, or feed them. Maybe we'll even go see Daddy in the shop behind the house.

Thank you, Dear Reader, for coming with me on this ride. Whether this is your first book penned by moi or you're already in my tribe and waiting for more, you uplift me. And frankly, I do this all for you.

And finally, thank you, Universe. Years ago, as I spiralled down my darkest rabbit hole ever, someone told me to write "The Universe has my back" on sticky notes and paste them on mirrors and door jams. And it helped. So thank you for that, and thank you for being ready when I was finally able to rise, shake it off, and discover myself and my happiness once and for all.

Thank you.

Introduction

It started innocently enough.

"I want to be the man in the caboose!" I told my parents when I was five, sitting in the back of our family car as we idled behind the railroad crossing's blinking lights.

"Why?" my mom asked from the passenger seat, turning to look quizzically over her sunglasses.

"Because he waves at everyone!" I replied. Could there be a better job than passing intersection after intersection, waving at passengers in cars and seeing them wave back? I didn't think so.

"I want to be a stripper when I grow up!" I excitedly told my mom, perched on the stairs leading to the front door. I'd been sitting there for what seemed like hours, eagerly waiting for her to come home so I could share my BIG NEWS the moment she stepped inside.

"Why?!" she asked me as she put down the groceries, half laughing, half concerned over the dissolving innocence of her six year old child.

"Because they go on a stage and everyone pays attention. It's so neat!"

I'd been flipping through the channels on a Saturday afternoon looking for something to watch and had come across an old black and white movie featuring Sally Rand. Falling on the scene moments before she entered for her signature peek-a-boo dance behind massive feather fans, the audience in formal gowns, tuxedos and top hats caught my attention with their excited hum. As she stepped onto the stage I wondered what could be better than capturing the attention of an entire room?

"I want to be a veterinarian when I grow up!" I proclaimed at 10, interrupting my parents after dinner TV time to announce my newest passion.

"Why?" my mom asked, looking up from her plate of cookies.

"Because they help animals," I replied. Helping living beings that were suffering and making them feel better appealed to me, calling out to the depths of my soul. By then I was aware I had an unusual gift; an ability to break through a creature's fears and become trusted in its space. I loved petting every furry animal I came across, and people often expressed surprise at how quickly the shy ones learned to cuddle up to me.

I tell people the Universe is always showing me my next two steps. Steps I don't always understand in the moment but feel compelled to take anyway. Steps that make sense only much later when I look back and see how that moment, that decision, led me to where I am today.

I use the word "compelled" a lot when I talk about what I do. I was compelled to buy a guide on publishing a book long before I ever attempted to write my first one. Compelled to move to Montreal, where I'd meet the girl who introduced me to the guy I moved to Ontario for, putting me on a path to meet my current husband and soulmate. Compelled to buy a greeting card depicting a wild haired girl perched on a stool, on her chest a whimsical image of a road weaving its way up from a dirt brown base, carving into lush green mountains before disappearing into a purple sky filled with fluffy clouds. The script writing encircling her reads, "If I could just sit still I know I could go far." I always understood that card spoke my destiny. To eventually sit still and then go far.

Which is where I now find myself. Nothing could be more still than this peaceful life on a quiet country road, pushing out words that inspire others around the world to live their own better life.

My husband and I, after years of unrest, have also found stillness together. And that quieting of our issues unleashed my creative explosion. A fiery concoction of clarity, drive, and passion rushed forth the moment my calmed mind was finally able to take all my ingredients, mix them together, and create magic.

There really is something magical that happens when love becomes settled. A releasing of sorts. See, when you can not only hear that voice in your head but actually lean into it as well, welcoming its message and taking the actions it pushes to the forefront of your mind, you begin to understand your own tapestry.

You know that forest for the trees saying? How standing too close to one tree will keep you from seeing the vastness behind it? You are cut the same way, my Dear Reader. You have so many threads woven into you, trailing into directions you can't even fathom yet. There are connections waiting to happen, inspirations waiting to be acknowledged, and beautiful designs straining to come together.

But maybe you're stuck staring at that one thread.

Maybe that thread is anxiety. Centering around your relationship perhaps? Or your stressful job, acting out kids, or your parents' health issues. Maybe there's a part of your soul that knows there's more out there for you past this one thread pulling at your focus, and you're aching to lean back and take a look at the design. *Your whole design.*

You hear a whisper at the back of your mind, saying "I'm meant for so much more." You know you have a talent, something you do exceptionally well. You feel a frustration any time you don't get to exercise that talent. You wonder if life is really 95% taking care of mundane stuff, 3% enjoyment, and 2% getting to use that part of you that makes you feel magical.

You hope maybe someday you'll have time to delve into your tapestry, allow it to be seen, experienced, loved, and appreciated. You dream of a time when you can open yourself up enough to actually see all of you. The part of you that gives what you love, and loves what you give.

And you're thinking right now that you're feeling ready. Ready to start examining those other threads, following them and seeing how they're woven. Ready to start sharing the talents inside you. To get beyond the functional pieces that work and sacrifice to help keep others afloat, and light up the golden parts that pull magic from deep inside you, coming through in glimmering accents that sparkle and shine and add a special element that is uniquely you.

You're ready to tap into your gift. That thing you're custom made to do.

Good, I say. Let's get this party started.

Love
is our
oxygen.

First Thing First

Free your mind, and your zeal will follow

Chapter 1

Fix Your Love

I'd be careless if I didn't start this book with the golden key to the depths of your soul. Because just like getting into a great relationship begins with purging your last one, beginning the ultimate relationship with your inner light takes some cleaning house too.

The fact is, if your brain is loaded down with negativity, it's hard to pull it towards a higher goal. It takes a lot of mental power to create goodness in your life, regardless of what you're pursuing. Whether you're going from single to in love, from fighting to peaceful with your partner, or from ordinary to lighting yourself up and making that inner fire a reality, you need to understand that the more your mind is at peace, the easier it becomes to choose functional behaviours that advance your goals.

My goal here, as it's always been, is to put a flashlight into your hands so you stop crashing around in the dark. "Look at the path; see how well paved and easy it is?"

And it does become easy when you gain perspective and really understand the ideal order of things. When you're looking for love in any form, whether it's romantic relationships or falling in love with the work you do, you need to settle into the functionality of love if you want to properly exercise it. And as always, what we're talking about is massive amounts of self-love.

"Self love? Chantal, I thought we were going to talk about finding my passion?!" Yes, my Dear Reader, we certainly are! But my # 1 relationship rule is, it's not fair to ask for anything you're not willing to do first. So if you want to bring forth what the world will love to receive from you, you've got to understand how to deposit that love inside yourself first.

If you're going to ask anyone to buy into your talent, to invest their time, money, and emotion, then you've got to set the tone by creating a beautiful gift that glows with your love-inspired energy. Because you won't stand out in a crowd if you're afraid to flip the switch and light your beacon first.

There are a ton of people out there starting businesses. The internet, in all its glorious freedom, is quickly being populated with start-ups, and it's gold rush time. But what will make *you* the one people find? What will make you distinct? It's love, my dear. Pure, shining, passionate love flowing from deep inside and infecting those who need your talent. Love will draw them in like a magnet because fundamentally love is what we are. It's what we seek, and it's what we inhale in order to survive.

And you, my Dear Reader, can contribute oxygen into this world, but first you've got to understand how.

Now, if you've already got your love life in order, you actually don't need this chapter. Either you've found a great partner and have a relationship that's supportive and free from fights, or you're single and perfectly happy. If your mind isn't entangled in the question "How can I fix the issues that are hurting my heart", you're good to go. Proceed to Step 1.

But if you're spinning when it comes to love, spending too much time trying to work out how you'll make things better, I want you to know once you settle that part of your life the rest of this book will be much easier to follow through on.

See, love is, in reality, rocket fuel for life. Whether it's the love you create in a relationship or the warm fuzzy glow you get from waking up each morning and appreciating your existence, when love is peaceful you gain a massive ability to expand outward. Why? Because you're not spinning inwardly.

Listen, we are always in movement. But if your mental movement is constantly being sucked into a vortex of issues, you're functioning with a limited amount of capacity. So why make lighting your inner fire harder than it needs to be?

Don't waste any time convincing yourself that you can forgo this step and everything will be just as easy. Ever hear the saying "You don't know what you don't know"? I've gained enough experience to understand that if I want to conquer this world, not just survive it, I've got to maintain focus and keep my mind as free from conflict as possible. Because the freer my mind is, the more I can use it productively.

The first time I became conscious of how much love affected my output was when I was studying social sciences in University. There was no way I was going to be paying for school and investing my time if I wasn't gonna to be a nerd and aim for top grades. But fighting with my man kept getting in the way. I'd be studying for an exam and realize I'd read the same page for the last five minutes, and still had no idea what was on it.

But I lacked conflict resolution tools. So what did I do? I basically stopped talking to my partner just to avoid fighting with him. It wasn't the greatest solution, but it was the only way I could stop my mind from desperately trying to fix our love life. In essence, I shelved my relationship so I could focus on what I wanted to achieve, choosing to sacrifice one for the other.

The second time I tried taking my inner fire to the next level I was *still* fighting with my husband. And once again I was at a crossroads; either focus on developing my business or spin inside my relationship. But I couldn't handle both simultaneously. So this time, instead of verbally shutting down I said straight out, "I can't do this. I can't handle trying to write a book and seminar on love while fighting so much with you. I need space." And my husband, in what seemed like a win-win situation for both of us, moved into his shop and began sleeping there. In essence, we separated.

And having him out of my space and out of my life helped. I stopped worrying about what I would say to change things. I stopped stressing about how I was going to fix both our heads instead of just mine. I even started to accept the fact that I might be one of those Dating Coaches who was single and hoped that all the theory and information I put out would override my one glaring discrepancy – that I could talk to you about love, but I couldn't set the example yet.

In hindsight though, we needed that break. He needed time and focus to expand his own business and to quit worrying about me and how we were reacting to each other for a while. And I needed space to work on myself and begin a self-love routine that would heal my brain and ease up on the incessant chatter happening inside my skull. He needed time to forget about our troubles, and I needed space to learn how to fix them.

This mini-vacation from each other was lifesaving for us. Why? Because instead of sitting back and allowing this downward spiral to continue I took that silence and leaned in. And do you know what I heard? My inner voice. My compass.

"Here," it said. "Check out this article by Harvard about meditation. It's what you need."

And it was so right.

"Listen," my inner voice told me. "You've got to get into your feelings and express them. Stop stuffing them down, because you're dying in your own poison."

Boy, was it right again.

"Stop thinking your anger is an indication that you're right. Question yourself. Recognize your ego and tell it to fuck off. Your ego is messing up your life right now."

Yup. Right again.

"Let me give you some tools that will facilitate love for you."

Mmmmm. Wow, that sure worked!

"You are strong enough now. Take your turn being the pillar of support in your relationship. Everything will be okay."

Was it ever spot on.

"Baby," I told my husband. "Come back home."

And as efficiently as I'd done for myself, I etch-a-sketched my husband's mind of all the negativity that had accumulated throughout our years of fighting. I created peace, first within myself, then within my relationship, then inside my husband's heart and head.

I healed, created functional love, spread that shit around, and the next thing I knew I was turbo charged.

I have a visual for what happens when you begin your passion project from a place where love is solid as a rock in your life. It's the same image that's on the cover of the Pink Floyd *Dark Side Of the Moon* album cover. Picture this; a triangle pierced with a bright white light on one side, emanating a brilliant rainbow out the other. You are the triangle, Dear Reader. The love being fed in you is that white light, and the source doesn't matter. It could be self-love, it could be the love you're showered with in your romantic relationship. Regardless of where that white light comes from, what's spilling from you is what the world will receive.

Rainbow coloured, supercharged, enhanced with your talent, love.

Delivered in whatever form you discover deep inside you. You could be feeding the world love though your accounting business. Your meal prep business. Your website development or MLM business. Whatever you put forth, the defining feature that'll make you shine above all the rest will be the amount of love projected along with it.

Listen, there are so many people sleep walking their way through their work. They think creating a product and putting it on a platform will generate the customers they want. But they're one in a bazillion. They're not distinct, and most of them will give up because they're not lit up with love. Their passion isn't red hot, it's just simmering.

But when someone steps out into the world glowing like a mo-fo, people take notice. Your product looks different because what you put into it isn't the same energy as everyone else. And ultimately, because love is a fuel, you'll outlast the people who can't withstand the time and emotional investment it takes to bring inner light from concept to reality, and from there to success.

So let's get back to the title of this chapter – first thing you've got to do is fix love and free your mind. Here is my recommendation: Read one (or more) of my books.

If you're spinning over your recent break up, read *Comeback Queen* and find your heart again. If you're spinning on your singledom and are on a dating hamster wheel, read *No More Assholes* and learn what a vetting process actually looks like. If you're fighting with your current partner and know deep down it could be so good, if only life's B.S stopped getting in the way, read *Fix That Shit* to get past the fighting and into the glorious beauty that love truly has to offer.

Free your mind, so your zeal can follow. Let that light, that bright white shining light of love, hit you straight on and fill you till you overflow, spilling out a rainbow of love. Let yourself become *lit*, so you can then turn around and light up those who will seek your product. Infect them with love, and watch as they turn and infect those around them.

In essence, don't sell them your product. Sell them your fire.

Exercise: List 3 ways you can create more love in your life.

_____

_____

_____

_____

_____

_____

_____

Journal: *Answer this question:* What's holding me back from creating more functional love for myself?

_____

_____

_____

_____

_____

_____

_____

_____

_____

_____

_____

_____

_____

_____

_____

_____

_____

_____

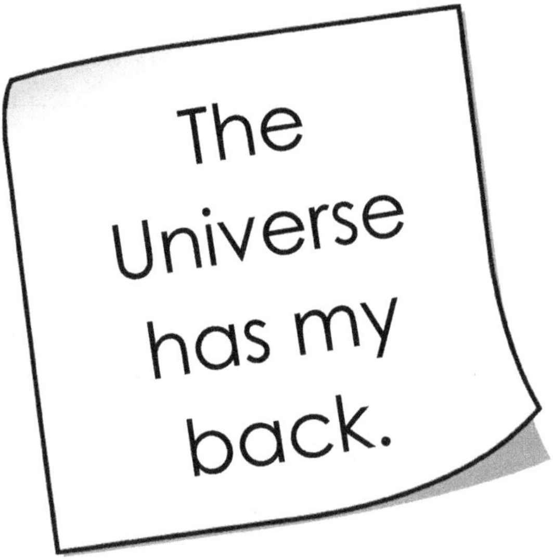
The Universe has my back.

Step 1 – Grounding

It's time to tap into your inner voice.

Chapter 2

The Importance of a Liberated Mind

Are you aware of how much chatter is going on inside your head? Do you know how much time you actually spend in the moment instead of off in the past rehashing, in the future anticipating, or somewhere in your own imagination creating checklists, scenarios, and conversations?

Are you realizing how much of your brain power is spent spinning on issues? Filling itself up with the things you didn't like, the things you hope won't happen, the things that might happen and how you'll deal with them when they do?

The things you need to do, haven't done, will hopefully do, and hope you won't have to do?

About that person who ticked you off each time you were in their presence, and how you wish they would just get their comeuppance already? The one you really need to say something to and your discomfort every time you think about how and when, which is so often it's become hard to even get off that runaway train of thought?

It's time to get conscious about what's going on inside your head. Look, before a massive change can take place in your outer world you've got to first get proficient at controlling your inner world. Because, Dear Reader, you're either the puppet or the puppet master. So who's going to pull your strings? All these whirling thoughts? Or you?

Now, I often say life begins when you ask the right question, and the right one always has an element of self-control.

"Why am I always feeling so anxious and pre-occupied?" you might ask. But let me draw you towards a better question. *Why are you letting yourself be carried away by your runaway brain?*

"Why does so-and-so piss me off so much?" How about this question instead: *Why are you letting so-and-so occupy so much of your brain space that you're reducing your capacities for awesomeness?* Personally, my mantra when I find myself spinning on something negative is, "how can I make better use of my brain?" Then I get to work on the first thing that pops up. Voila! I've taken the strings and directing myself once again.

So why are you letting life control you instead of taking the wheel and driving destiny yourself? Simple question, isn't it?

"The simplest solution tends to be the best one," states a philosophy called Occam's Razor. And so with that in mind let me propose something radical. Once you gain control of your mind, very little in life will feel beyond your control.

Not your love life, not your career, not your friendships, and most important of all, not your well-being. Knowing how to focus your brain is key to unlocking everything you've ever wanted. Peace, ambition, love, and success will be in the palm of your hand. But if you want all that, you've got to start at the top.

Inside your head.

Think about it. You're reading this book because you've got questions in mind: How can I figure out what my passion is? How can I take this idea I have, and take it to the next level? How can I find the ambition, the energy, and the focus I need to take these concepts and turn them into reality?

It's easier than you think. Simpler than you think. Because that's how Mother Nature functions. She feeds you simplicity, and it's up to you to grasp her concept and make it work for you.

So let's start with that beautiful mind of yours. Let's unlock what's inside and slide into the ease of letting your light spill out and infect the world with Goodness. I know you're primed, I know you're mentally fist pumping the air because you're so eager. I know you're like a race horse straining at the gate, ready to take off the moment those doors open. And I know you're finally willing to unleash the sweet spot inside your soul and watch it grow and evolve until you shake your head in wonder at how fulfilling this ultimate liberty is.

I know you feel something growing inside you, like a gestating baby getting bigger and bigger until it's filling you up with its sensation of need. "Let's do this" it's saying. "Let's take our talent and change the world."

So you know what? Let's make this growing passion your focus. Never mind those past or future scenarios. Never mind the negative people who take up too much of your attention. Never mind all those endless spinning moments.

Never mind. You've got better things to do with your brain now.

Exercise: List 3 things that occupy your mind too much.

_____

_____

_____

_____

_____

_____

_____

Journal: *Answer this question:* My mind doesn't *need* to spin on these things because _____.

_____

_____

_____

_____

Chapter 3

Meditation Is Your Salve

"How can I free my mind when so much is going wrong in my life?"

Great question! Let me introduce you to the one thing that mental freedom easier. The thing that reduces mindless spinning, reduces anxiety, reduces fear, and calms your brain enough to help you find real solutions. The one activity that gives you better relationship tools, keeps fights with others at bay, and magnetically attracts more of the support you need.

Side effects include liking people more. Liking yourself more. Increased focus. And an ability to hear the voice that will be your ultimate guide on this journey.

Meditation is your #1 tool on the trip you're about to embark on. I mean, you can skip this chapter, skip making meditation a part of your life, skip forward and do the rest of the exercises in this book. But let me ask you this. Do you want to make this easy? Or do you want it to be hard?

Because you're standing at that exact crossroad right now. Choosing to ignore what I teach in this section, to not make meditation a part of your life by creating a habit that's as routine as brushing your teeth is a choice to trudge uphill rather than take the easy route.

Seriously.

Before I started meditating I couldn't pull myself out of a depression and addiction rut that lasted for years. Before meditating my relationship was in shambles, and all my husband and I did was go from one fight to the next. Before I started meditating the book growing inside my belly kept eluding me, ending up in one failed attempt after another.

Once I started meditating, though, I quit fighting with my husband and taught him to stop too. I reduced my anxiety, halted my downward spiral, and shelved the alcohol and hard drugs I was using in my misguided attempts to quell dysfunctional thoughts and difficult emotions.

Once I started meditating I heard the voice in my head switch from telling me "It's okay, you'll make it through this, and you'll teach what you learn" to "This is the lesson. This is your talent. This is your first seminar, your first book, your branding, and your unique message."

See, once I started meditating I went from survival mode to thriving mode. And awesomeness began to spill out of me at a pace that was hard to keep up with.

I credit meditation for my peace of mind, yes. But I also credit it for my ability to write seven books over the course of three years. With my ability to show up at book signings, trade shows, and public speaking events almost every weekend for a full year. I credit it for helping me keep my serenity while I built a business from the ground up and got myself recognized as a voice of reason in my industry.

I credit meditation for my life. For the fact that I still exist today and am now changing women's lives while helping them change the lives of those around them. I cannot stress enough how much you need this step. I cannot explain enough how much this one thing will help you be successful. You'll have to find out for yourself.

So let me make it easy for you.

"I can't meditate! I've tried and I just can't do it. I don't have time. I can't stop my mind from thinking. I get stressed out when I try."

Shhhhhh…. You haven't done it the Chantal way. It's easier than you think. Can you sit in a chair? Wear headphones? Close your eyes? Yes? Good, then you can meditate!

This notion that you have to clear your mind is B.S. You don't. In fact, I think a lot when I meditate. I have little conversations with the Universe. I imagine, create, and then say Thank You for what's been good and what's going to be good. Meditation is soil, my friend. Rich, black, nutrient dense soil that you get to plant seeds into and watch grow into massive forests of Goodness. It's awesomeness, right up inside your head. And it's the best thing that will ever happen to you.

Do you have a comfy spot for meditation inside your home? Yeah, you do; it's called your living room couch. Do you have headphones? Of course you do, and if you don't, go spend twenty bucks and buy a pair; you'll need them for the kind of meditation tracks I'm going to turn you on to. Do you have eyelids? Of course you do.

So now, checklist completed, it's time to start meditating.

My editor Kit always tells me I should be using hyperlinks instead of what I'm about to say next, but I'm a believer in the power of action and I want you to consciously do these next steps. Let's wire then into your brain so you can repeat them anytime, anywhere, on any device. Ready?

Go to YouTube. Search my name. Find my channel and then find my Let's Meditate playlist. You're going to find a video at the very top that shows you just how easy it is to sit in a chair and close your eyes. Then you're going to grab your headphones, plug them into whatever you're using, and if you're not drawn to anything else listen to the 10 minute Love Frequency.

Almost all of the tracks you'll find on my Let's Meditate playlist are infused with what's called Binaural Beats. These are basically frequencies that help pull your brain into a meditative state faster, helping you make those precious minutes even more effective and efficient. Because every minute counts, am I right, busy Mammas and Pappas?

If what I just said sounds like a bunch of mumbo-jumbo, let me paint a clearer picture for you. Ever see someone sitting in a chair with electrodes all over their head while a monitor shows wavy lines? What's being measured is the frequency emitting from their brains. You've heard the words Alpha, Beta, Theta, Delta? These are all states of frequency your mind can experience at in any given time, depending on your activity.

Right now, as you read this, your brain is emitting Beta waves of frequency. Go to sleep and start dreaming, and you'll slip into your Theta waves. Fall deeper into sleep, beyond dreams, and you're now entering the Delta zone. But the one you'll achieve when you start meditating is an Alpha state of mind. Cool name, right? And so on point. Cause once you start tapping into your Alpha brainwaves some pretty neat stuff is going to start happening.

We've been fooled into thinking life is difficult, but it's time to unplug from all the unconscious messaging infiltrating your psyche and complicating things. No, relationships aren't hard; it's your anxiety that makes them feel hard. No, feeling peaceful isn't hard, it's all the negative messages bombarding you from every media outlet that makes it feel hard. No, uncovering your passion and putting it into action isn't hard. It's all the jumbled up thoughts ramming your consciousness and putting you into overdrive that makes it feel hard to tap into, understand, and tackle in a way that not only feels right but fun too.

It's all easier than you think. You just need to start at the right place. Am I saying this enough?

So here's your homework. You're going to get in an average of at least 10 minutes a day. Should you want to do more, do more! But your minimum is 10 minutes daily. I know, you'll skip days here and there, which is fine. Look, we all get crazy busy sometimes. But by day 3 things will ease up and you're going to sit down and do 30 minutes to catch up. Capiche?

You're going to draw up an 8 week calendar and put in on your fridge. You're going to write in the number of minutes you meditate each day, and tally up your weekly average. And you're going to get more diligent the next week if you find yourself falling below your daily average this week.

You're going to make meditation your habit cause you're going to fall in love with what happens next. Once you realize how much your fear and anxiety go down with meditation and your mental clarity is unleashed, you'll never want to go back to your old brain again,

Old brain? Well, yes actually. Your reduction in negative feelings and increase in productive thoughts and ambition don't just happen, they're a result of how your brain will actually change in structure.

See, Harvard University did a study. They had participants come in and submit to an MRI scan, go home and meditate for 8 weeks, then come in for another MRI scan. And guess what they found? The participants' area responsible for fight or flight, the amygdala, shrunk. And the part where their compassion, introspection, and memory stem from, called the hippocampus, increased in size by creating more grey matter. See? New brain.

A superhero brain. The kind of brain you need to conquer the crap out of life. The sort of brain that's free from mundane, repetitive thoughts about shit you can't do anything about. The kind of brain that makes you feel more peaceful and creates more peace in those around you because you stop contributing to negativity. A brain equipped to bring forth the Goodness that's deep inside you, figure out the steps for turning it into reality, and get 'er done.

Exercise: Create an 8 week meditation chart and put it on your fridge. Then fill it in. Days where you don't meditate get a X. Write the daily number of minutes you do meditate, whether it's 37 or 2, or keep track of your minutes below. Every minute counts!

_____

_____

_____

_____

_____

_____

_____

_____

Journal: _Answer these questions:_ What are my excuses for not meditating? How will I overcome them?

_____

_____

_____

_____

_____

Chapter 4

How To "Use" Meditation

Let me make sure you fully understand that I am not insane. I do not, under any circumstance, expect you to sit in a chair for 10 minutes with a completely blank mind.

Instead, I want you to harness the power of your thoughts and imagination. To use them to your advantage. So I'm going to teach you a couple of tricks here; one I call the *redirect*, and the other is *manifesting with your imagination*.

First, the redirect. Of course your mind will run off on you, it's used to doing that. It's up to you to catch it and send it in the direction you actually want it to go in. Key word here is "catch".

So grab your butterfly net, and every time you realize you're in a thought that's negative and distracting you from your goal, it's time to do some catching. Trap it in your net, stuff it in a bottle (sealed with an alcohol soaked wad of cotton cause there's no point letting it live), and interrupt your train of thought with something more functional for you.

Don't know what to think instead? Then use this simple rule: If you don't like where your mind is, then find the opposite of what's happening up there.

"I'm not smart enough/good enough/talented enough" can be replaced with "I'm amazing at what I offer, and people appreciate what my gift does for them."

"I'm so mad about (fill in the blank)" can be redirected to "I'm so grateful and happy about (my past, present, and future achievements)."

In essence, keep realizing what's happening inside your head and keep pushing your thoughts towards functional rather than dysfunctional notions. All. The. Time. I'm serious when I say you'll do this a million times a day if you're doing this right. You've spent far too much time letting your thoughts run you; it's now time for you to run your thoughts.

Now, I'm talking about this step in a chapter about meditation, and you'll indeed do this a lot during your (minimum) 10 minute sessions, but I want you to do this throughout your day too. Every day, every night, every moment, catch yourself. Be cognizant of what's happening inside your head and redirect it if it's negative. You're on a mission to create awesomeness in your life, and this tool is part of your master plan.

The second thing you should employ during meditation sessions is your imagination. What is your desired outcomes? What do you want to see appear in your life? What will help your business succeed?

My business is about writing and teaching, so I'll picture an arena full of women holding my books high in the air, proudly showing off what helped change their lives. Or walking out onto a massive stadium stage and being welcomed by thousands of women who love all the happiness I've helped them create.

Listen, no dream is too big, and if you dream too small you risk never achieving half the success you could.

So unleash your imagination when you're sitting with those headphones on and changing the structure of your mind. Keep putting yourself into the space you actually want to end up in. Create a crystal clear picture of what massive success looks like for you. And if you only reach half that goal you're still much further along than if you'd never bothered to dream at all.

Exercise: List one to three major goals.

_____

_____

_____

_____

_____

_____

_____

_____

Journal: Describe your major goals in detail. What do you see around you? What do you hear? Smell? Taste? Write the scenes as though you were living them.

_____

_____

_____

_____

Chapter 5

Say Yes to Your Potential

It may well happen that beginning this journey with meditation will blow your mind. It sure blew mine.

It's not uncommon for meditation to start unlocking visions and experiences that are out of this world. You may see images that seem like future broadcasts of your life. You might travel to unworldly places. You might feel yourself achieve new levels, both emotionally and spiritually.

It's important to relax and accept these as they come, because the last thing you want to do is reject the Goodness your psyche is directing your way. Messages will be seeping through in all sorts of ways, and being receptive both in your meditative mind and everyday experiences will create a double whammy of elevation that can propel you and keep you pointed in the right direction.

You may find yourself at a crossroads moment inside your mind like I did. Early on, during one of my meditation sessions I got hit by a vibrant "view" of a beautiful, sunny backyard complete with a wide marble patio, rattan lounging furniture, and lush green grass that gently sloped to calm blue waters.

"Do you accept?" the voice in my head asked, and I understood – I had a choice to make. I could accept or reject this vision, but whichever path I chose in that moment would help pave the way to my future.

"Yes" I said, and I was immediately overcome by tears of pure joy. In a way, this was probably the moment the phrase *Say Yes to Goodness* was born.

You might get whisked up and away to have a deeper conversation with that voice inside your head. A few times I ended up in space, floating among the stars while wisdom wove itself inside my mind. During one of those visits I learned that everything happens "because of Love", and I came back with a better understanding that even the negatives in life are borne from a want of love, as dysfunctional as that can be at times.

Another occurrence happens when your entire frequency shifts. I call those moments "levelling up".

There's a video by Deepak Chopra I like to watch once or twice a year. He talks about the seven levels of spiritual ascension, and the first three are easily understood by most. Number one is deep, dreamless sleep, where you're not dead but you're not experiencing any conscious awareness either. The second is REM sleep, where inside your dreaming mind you're experiencing an understanding of yourself taking space and the existence of others around you.

The third state takes place in this physical world. Here, you look back at your dream state and say, "Huh. All that seemed real, but it was just a dream, and *this here* is real life."

But then you start meditating, and within that journey begin unlocking the next four levels. I like to re-watch this video as time goes by, because with each replay I realize my unfolding experiences are signaling how much I'm levelling up.

It's weird and exciting all at once.

The fact is you *will* change. Your emotional world will change, and so will your experiences. If you take on meditation and don't stop, you're in for a helluva ride. What I want you to do is trust it.

I want you to compare this experience to going to school. When you first step into the classroom you're playing with blocks and learning your ABCs and 123s. But as your brain develops, your education does too, giving you not just more information, but more deeply developed ideas too.

You'll go from pointing to the dog saying "dog", to spelling dog, to asking "If a dog barks in the woods and nobody hears it, is it still a bad dog?"

Meditation offers you that same educational ascension, feeding you everything your developing mind can handle. The more you meditate, the more intricate knowledge will begin to infiltrate your everyday experiences. Take it, and run with it. It's a gift to you from the Universe, your reward for doing something incredibly powerful for yourself.

Exercise: List three things you hope will shift because you're meditating.

_____

_____

_____

_____

_____

_____

_____

Journal: *Fill in the blank:* When I come across people who meditate I'm impressed by their _____.

_____

_____

_____

_____

_____

_____

_____

_____

_____

Step 2 – Clarity

Your story will unlock your insights.

Chapter 6

There Will Be Clues

Some of you are holding this book because you're already aware of what's lighting you up and want guidance lifting that passion from concept to execution. Good, you'll find that here for sure! But some of you are trying to dig through mounds of outside influences clogging up your mind, looking to find the beautiful talent buried deep inside. That's what this chapter is all about.

The fact is there's a timeless part of you that pretty much knows everything. Your past, your future, it's all in you already, and all you need to do is get out that big ol' magnifying glass so you can see a little clearer.

There were things you really wanted to do once. Things you dabbled in and either dismissed, stopped, or outright failed at. Maybe some of them are cringe worthy fails. I'll never forget the time I was asked to give a presentation to 200 students at a University, and ended up learning the hard way how to talk to a crowd. Standing in front of a large group engrossed in their cell phones while I shakily bombed my way through Power Point slides and awkward silences really taught me how to NOT command a stage. Worse yet, I'd asked my boyfriend to come see me in action. See, cringe worthy.

But those things you've failed at in your past? Well, consider them prep work. They prepared you for your next steps by weaving their possibility into your mind. I learned I could stand in front of 200 people, and I just needed to fine tune things the next time around.

Whatever you do, don't discount something just because you sucked at it before. Suckage has nothing to do with talent; suckage is actually part of the process when developing yourself in any facet of life. So as we take this trip through history to find what your true gift to the world is, take the word "failure" and toss it out the window. It's irrelevant here.

That being said, let's look for those clues now.

Let's go really far back. I mean as far as around 5 to 8 years old. You might find some clues there, and they're worth taking stock. What were you naturally good at as a child?

One of the things I try to help kids and teens understand is the wrongness they'll encounter in our educational system. Let me explain before your head explodes.

When you go to school they give you grades based on your work. "You're great at that, here's your star. But you suck at this, so spend more time, work harder, focus more, and really develop this part so you get much better." Unfortunately, this is one of the ways we're told to forget about what lights us up and focus on what doesn't.

"Here's your yearly employee review," your boss will say once you leave school and get a job. "You're great at that, but not so good in this area. So put some more time, focus, and energy in improving this, and hopefully I'll have something better to say at your next review."

See what happened here? We took our school experience as a child and, because we repeat what's familiar even if it's wrong for us, found ourselves in another environment that emulated exactly what we'd been taught. To ignore our strengths and focus on our weaknesses.

Well, not today, Satan.

Close your eyes and imagine your tiny self again. Relax into the memory of what you did when nobody was paying attention and you just wanted to occupy your time. What were you drawn to? What felt easy for you?

My thing was animals. If it lived and had fur, it was a magnet for me. If it was scared, no problem. I had the time, patience, and most importantly, enough intuition to break down fears and get my little hands on it.

Any kitties hiding under beds at houses we visited.

The abused Cocker Spaniel my neighbor adopted that would only allow four people close enough to pet her silky fur. The three who fed her and me.

The scared dog at the shelter (I did community service when I got caught being a bad teenager) that only let me leash and walk him.

When it came to gaining trust I was always as natural as Snow White, and I now get to put that talent into play every time someone tells me their story in exchange for a solution to their problems.

Your next clues lie in the things you chose to do as a teen. What kind of activities were you drawn to? You'll find your prep work in those things that seem like here today, gone tomorrow notions. If you were following your heart they may well have been your early stepping stones. What kind of classes did you sign up for "just for fun"?

At 14 I decided to take a modelling course at our community college. I was a nerd in the worst sense of the word, and I wanted to start shedding my awkwardness so I could step into a better version of myself. We made oatmeal and honey face masks and walked with books on our heads, and when that class ended I sought out an even more advanced version. Taught by a young woman with experience in photo shoots and runway shows, I learned how to strut my way through life and say "Thank you" when someone gave me a compliment, even if I felt uncomfortable. Combined, these two experiences helped me develop the self-esteem I'd need to step in front of people and allow myself to be judged with my head held high.

Then there was that time, at 16, when I entered a lip-sync competition. For weeks Lee Aaron's "Whatcha Do to My Body" played on repeat in my Walkman as I worked hard to memorize it, and despite being super nervous, I fluffed up my hair, put on my shortest miniskirt, and pretended I was a rock and roll goddess. I came away from that experience feeling like if I could do *that*, there wasn't anything I couldn't muster up the courage to tackle.

Notice how those events correspond to the fact that today I regularly get up on stages, showing off my "talent" to groups? And how my "here kitty, kitty, kitty" ability translates into building a business where entire families look to me for guidance? Your teens and twenties are when you're subconsciously setting the foundation for the gift you'll be unleashing later on in life. All these seemingly unrelated things you experienced will ultimately become puzzle pieces inside your bigger picture. I see my talent was evident *then*, I got my confidence *there*, and I gained more courage *here*.

The third part I want you to look at is your so-called failures. Those are the things you had the balls to try because not doing them seemed worse. "Try this, or risk regretting not doing it." No fear was too big for those huge tasks, and crashing and failing wasn't part of the plan because you were too preoccupied with making it happen.

My big doozy was opening a health food store in my early 30s. In what I'll call my "first attempt to change the world" I was a hard-core vegan, aiming to save the planet and every living being on it. This was my biggest challenge and my mightiest loss, but the lesson I gleaned from it all is crystal clear. I'm designed to want nothing less than life saving evolution for all of us.

I'll risk being ridiculed for my weird ways and my different philosophies. I'll risk making a fool of myself on stages. But my heart and soul strive for positive change, and I'll put everything on the line to try to make it happen.

So what are your clues? What was so natural to you as a child that you never even thought twice before doing it? What were you drawn to exploring when nobody but yourself was guiding your course of action? What were you so willing to do that it didn't even matter how much courage it took to show up?

I just got a shiver writing that paragraph.

I know those of you who were in the dark will begin to better understand yourselves right now. You don't have to sit and ask yourself what your passion or your talent is. You just have to look into your own history and find the bread crumbs you've left behind, guiding yourself back to the deepest, least indoctrinated, and purest parts of your psyche.

Exercise: List one to three talents you had as a child.

_____

_____

_____

_____

_____

_____

_____

Journal: *Answer these questions:* What have you tried and enjoyed in your past? What did you appreciate about that experience? What made you happy when you explored this?

_____

_____

_____

_____

_____

_____

Chapter 7

Have a Vision

Vision boards work.

It's the weirdest thing. I created my first board when my business was little more than a confused set of ideas, and I hadn't even written my first book yet. A friend of mine organized a vision boarding party and I thought, *What the hell, I've been playing with the idea for years anyway.* So I picked up every magazine I found, asked around for more, and, I confess, stole a few from waiting rooms.

I cut out images of homes surrounded by forests, spacious kitchens, and bookshelves filled with what would be *my* books. I carefully glued them onto my poster paper along with some motivational words, then rolled up my project and stuffed it in a corner of my office until I threw it out in a move.

I forgot what was on it and created three more in the years since, but a few months ago I was taking a walk down memory lane and thought about that board again. And you know what? I freaked out.

Because my vision had come about.

The house we moved into about a year later is surrounded by woods.

My kitchen is big.

My bookshelves now include seven books written by moi, and I'm on track to write two books a year for the next ten years.

My second vision board is just as alive, with reality jumping off the page and into my life. Image of "me" stylin' lush, fluffy hair? Check. Image of "me" on stage while people watch in rapt attention? Check. Image of "me" giving a Ted Talk? Check. (It was advertised as a "Ted Style Talk" but the match is there!) And smack dab in the middle of that board are the words "Tell your story". Check.

You've heard the saying "If you can conceive it, you can achieve it"? Well, there's magic behind those words.

See, you're a walking antennae, Dear Reader. At all times. You're like a cell phone, writing messages and sending them to an external tower, where they'll be relayed to whoever they're made for. This is why what's on your mind is vital to your future success. Think the wrong things, and you're complicating your future. Think the right ones, and you're facilitating.

It's as though your thoughts are magnetic.

Don't believe me? I'm not even sure you have to. I didn't hold much stock in my first vision board but, voila, it came to life anyway. My next one is prominently displayed in my office, and when I take photos from the past few years and hold them up to images on my board I can see that they're nearly identical.

Here's the thing: magic exists regardless of whether or not you believe in it. Just like oxygen, it's something we rarely think about but affects us anyway. You're constantly creating magic. Your only decision is whether it'll be beneficial magic, or, well, you can guess the alternative.

Discounting the power of your own imagination is like discounting how useful your thumbs are to everyday life. Don't make that mistake; instead, make a safer bet. Gamble on the notion that what's on your mind is being transmitted into your future, and make your vision board ASAP.

You just never know how quickly it'll come to life.

Here is your step by step guide to building your vision board:

Collect anything you can tear apart. Magazines of all sorts provide tons of content, so start collecting until you have about 15 to 20. Variety is the spice of life!

Cut out everything that catches your attention. Don't hold back! Some will make it on your board and some will go by the wayside, but letting your intuition guide you during this process is key, and now is a good time to start trusting yourself. Second guessing is for schmoes.

Don't limit yourself to just images. I've got a bunch of words and phrases pasted on my boards, which I love because they guide me. "Staying connected" reminds me to reach out to people after my public appearances. "Your year to shine" feels like a truth nugget every year. "I will light up every room I walk into" reminds me of my power to create positive change no matter where I go. "Invest" motivates me to keep giving back into my business and community in order to create even more growth.

Separate the tasks so it doesn't seem like such a big job. Sit down and flip through all your magazines in one shot, cutting out everything that speaks to you. Done. Next time you have time and feel motivated, go ahead and paste them on your cardboard.

When you do your pasting, don't think too much. Let your intuition guide what you put on and in what order you do it. Funny thing about my current vision board, it actually "reads" from left to right in columns. Yours might not pan out that way though, so follow your heart.

Vision board checklist:

- ✓ Large cardboard paper
- ✓ Magazines
- ✓ Scissors and glue (or tape)
- ✓ Get er' done attitude

Exercise: Create a vision board.

_____

_____

_____

_____

_____

_____

_____

_____

Journal: _Answer this question:_ What I hope to gain from my vision board is _____.

_____

_____

_____

_____

_____

_____

_____

_____

_____

_____

_____

_____

_____

Chapter 8

Let Your Ideas Develop Your Methods

Listen, there isn't a thing in this world that doesn't include evolution as part of its existence, and the same goes for how you'll develop your talent and turn it into a business.

If you compared my first photo shoot to my current image, you'll get an idea of how much change is involved in turning yourself into something close to a final product. And I say close, because once you find a comfortable spot to operate from you'll still be shifting your vision, just maybe at a slower pace compared to your early years.

"Progress, not perfection" is a great mantra for any stage in your life, but it's especially important to remember when you start putting yourself out there. Staying stuck trying to create the perfect logo, the perfect pitch, the perfect *you* before signing up for a business headshot will just keep you spinning, and you'll actually slow the pace of your growth.

Writing my eighth book in three years means I've got variety for my readers and am keeping them engaged with me. Sure, there are typos in my stuff. Sure there are formatting errors. Sure, some sentences are still too long, or maybe I leave an idea too abruptly before starting the next. But you know what? Not a single person has lodged a complaint. Instead, I get emails all the time from people who tell me they love my work, love what I have to say, and love what I'm helping them achieve in their lives.

"I bought your book last year and it helped me so much!" said the first person to arrive at my booth the second year I was peddling myself at a local trade show for women. I'd only had *No More Assholes* the previous year, but by the same time the following year I had *Comeback Queen*, *After The First Kiss*, and *Fix That Shit* on display alongside it. And she bought all three. So never hold yourself back, because you never know what your imperfect self will contribute to the world.

Your growth comes from allowing yourself to flow from one idea to the next, shedding old versions like a snake sheds a skin. Will you look back on your old stuff and cringe? Of course you will. So what? The people you collect early on will admire your ability to forge forward, while the people you collect in your later evolutions will never know. Frankly, I'm hoping those who bought a first edition of *No More Assholes* keep it. Who knows, it might be worth money one day!

Exercise: List one idea you're going to start working on this week without caring about quality first.

_____

_____

_____

_____

_____

Journal: Write a story depicting what people will love about what you create.

_____

_____

Chapter 9

10 Year Plan for Overnight Success

When it comes to businesses, especially homegrown ones sparked by an internal flame, there are a lot of starters but not a lot of finishers. Why? Because most people don't have realistic expectations.

Remember that fabulous line from the movie *Field Of Dreams*? "If you build it, they will come" stored itself deep in my dreamer's mind, and I never forgot those words. Unfortunately, not everything has a Hollywood ending, and simply building something doesn't mean you'll achieve success any time soon.

The fact is a common timeline to even seeing a business come out of the red is five years, and hopefully the climb upwards is continuous. But that all depends on (mostly) you.

Can you sustain your passion and drive? Is the fire inside burning so bright you keep feeding light onto the world regardless of obstacles, because not doing so is even more painful than quitting? I certainly feel that way. In fact, I started this whole thing just to ease the physical discomfort I felt when I ran out of people to help. I *had* to keep doing what I was doing, doling out perspective and information that helped women find and create the love they were yearning for or risk falling into an emotional black hole because what was making me feel alive had no outlet.

That spark you'll turn into a money-making inferno has to be something you'll want to do regardless of outcomes. There's a beautiful quote by Marsha Sinetar that perfectly describes what I'm talking about: "Do what you love, and the money will follow."

What she's touching on is the emotional aspect of business, something you need to take into account. If you can't operate from a perspective of pure passion, you'll never be able to ride the waves of disappointment that are bound to happen now and then. They'll drain your willingness to forge forward in dark times, broke times, lazy times, and confused times. You'll worry too much about attempts that fail to deliver rewards instead of focussing on your development and lessons. If you're so in love with what you offer that it doesn't even matter if nobody is buying in right now, you'll never lose your zest to evolve until you're as well-known as you need to be.

Can you put in the sweat equity? There's barely a minute of my day where I'm not working at my business in some form or another. Making modifications to my website, writing new books, creating blog posts and videos, tweaking my branding, talking to clients, booking appearances and showing up for them... the list goes on and on, and though none of it actually feels like work it truly is a helluva lot of effort. Do you have it in you to put in a sustained effort for the next 10 years?

Understand that what you're building should never be a house of cards, constructed in a few minutes and too flimsy to stand up to anything stronger than a light breeze. This is a marathon, my friend, not a sprint. You've got to dig that foundation, carefully lay the concrete, erect a sturdy frame, and lovingly build it up brick by brick. This takes energy over a long period of time, and you need to be up to the task of applying yourself every day.

Can you handle the flux and flow? The emotional roller coaster that comes with wondering if things will ever take off when you hit a lull? Do you believe in yourself enough to power through your moments of doubt? Because taking your talent and creating an income takes a lot of emotional strength, and a resistance to giving up before the rewards come in. Going from starter to finisher takes a huge amount of courage and self-esteem, and that's without taking into consideration the mental fuckery that happens when a business mistake results in a wave of regret.

Think of this as a relationship between you and your passion. You've got to be fair, not asking it to give you more than you're willing to give first. You've got to be consistent, able to choose functional courses of action and not give up on the hope that eventually they'll reward you with what you need. You've got to have clarity about your gifts and be able to have faith in your talents. And you've got to have patience, so you can see all your work eventually create the shift you're looking for.

And lastly, are you willing to give yourself 10 years to make it happen? Because perspective is everything. You can either say to yourself, "I've spent 3 years at this and I'm barely seeing results." Or you can say, "I'm at year 3 and look how far I've come!"

Listen, winning mindsets is no mistake. If you go and listen to anyone successful talk about their journey, one thing resonates across the board – they struggled and struggled, but never lost faith or took their eye off the ball. No siree, they didn't just work.

They worked *until*.

Until they got that big break. Until that first book was published. Until they got the recognition they'd worked so hard to earn.

And then they worked just as hard to sustain it, piggy backing their successes one on top of another to keep their momentum moving forward. But you'll never get to that point if you can't be okay with falling off your surf board every now and then, tumbling beneath the waves and fighting your way back to the surface so you can get back on to try again.

Life is full of ups and downs, and your business will be no different. But what'll make you stand out from the crowd will be your ability to outlast your competition. Your hutzpah will be your greatest asset, so dig deep and find it because you'll need your grit to get you to the ten year mark.

Exercise: List three qualities about yourself that make you strong.

_____

_____

_____

_____

_____

Journal: Write about a moment in your life where you learned you were stronger than you thought.

_____

_____

_____

_____

_____

_____

_____

_____

Chapter 10

Let Your Ideas Develop Your Method

Remember a minute ago when I said your business is like another relationship in your life? It's for this reason that you should give your heart a voice and let it lead the way. You want to stay in love, right? And we all know the #1 contributor to a relationship's death is emotional starvation, as a lack of love slowly deprives it of life until there's nothing left.

There are many things you'll need to do to get your business off the ground. You'll need to build a website, then create your social media platforms and draw your target audience in, not to mention figure out who your audience is. You'll maybe write a book so people understand you actually know what you're talking about, then go out and promote yourself like crazy. The list goes on and on.

It's. So. Much. Work.

And you'll find yourself stressing sometimes over the magnitude of your to-do list. Don't. Instead, take a deep breath, have a cup of tea, meditate, and then do the first thing you want to do because that's what'll be created with the loving energy that'll be oh-so-attractive to the right person.

You might have heard about experiments where people talk nice to one houseplant while being verbally abusive to the one next to it, and seen the drastic difference between the two. The one getting kindness thrived, while the one being bullied wilted. You need to be conscious about what kind of vibe you're putting into your work, so people feel it's as nourishing as those complimentary vibrations being soaked up like rays of sunshine.

So worry less about what you're doing, and do what you're going to love in the moment. Everything will come together in time, and once it's completed your audience will love it as much as you do.

Look, I'm a big fan of constant forward movement, no matter how small. I might have a hangover day and do nothing more than add a picture to Instagram. So what? I did it with heart and harbored no resentment about my efforts, which means at no point will my audience feel like they're a burden on me.

Understand that the order in which you achieve goals isn't the point right now. When your product is relatively done you'll have a larger picture that people can buy into, and they won't know if the chicken or the egg came first. Again, this is all about the long game, so tackle what's lighting your fancy when it does instead of forcing yourself to trudge miserably through this experience.

And don't forget there's a flip side of those low production days, and that's the no-sleep nights. I can't tell you how many times I finally crawled into bed at 4 am because I *needed* to unleash the ideas in my head. Respect your drive, and you'll make up for those lazy days by releasing your full force when your brain demands it.

I have days when I literally run back and forth from my office to the kitchen because I need to make food, but I don't want to interrupt the flow of work pouring out of me. My parents spent years having to be okay with me either not wanting to leave my house to visit or seeing me show up with my laptop and spend hours of my time with them wrapped up in work.

The fact is you've got to be good at giving yourself permission. Permission to work as much or as little as you want. Permission to start off with an image in mind and modify it a million times so it can evolve. Permission to make mistakes, to hit dead ends, to lose money, to start something over from scratch. To feel down or elated, to take stock of your successes, and to be okay with your failures (ugh, I so hate that word. It's sooo not a failure if it's a learning point.). Permission to dabble and try and experiment, and permission to delegate and outsource what falls outside your strengths.

But most importantly, permission to trust what's inside your head and heart. Because all this effort, as assbackwards as it might seem sometimes, (my first husband often pointed out that I start any new project in the *middle*) will eventually come together in a beautiful way, ultimately showing you the butterfly that was hiding inside your cocoon all along.

Exercise: List the time of day when you feel most productive.

_____

_____

_____

_____

Journal: _Answer this question:_ When it comes to being productive, what do you beat yourself up about the most? Then write a letter that forgives you and gives you permission to be yourself. End it with a commitment to create during your most productive time of day.

_____

_____

_____

_____

_____

_____

_____

Chapter 11

Don't Reinvent The Wheel

This is a rule that many business moguls will want to pound into you. If someone else has already figured out what works, why make things harder on yourself? Does it make sense to try finding an alternate way to achieve similar success?

Look, parts of your output are going to be pure creativity. That's your vision, your talent, your ability to change the world in some small or big way that's uniquely you. This is the part where nothing but pure imagination will come into play, and that's good. You need to be different; otherwise, you're just another voice getting lost in the babble.

But there are other areas of your business that won't require your creativity, like what you should keep in mind in order to reach a wider audience. Here is where you need to study others to find the winning formula. This is the part where you emulate rather than create from scratch.

How should you enter a room, approach people, and sell your product to strangers who've never heard of you? Find someone you admire in this area, study them, and imitate their confidence.

How should you direct your creative side, and what sort of output should you be pushing yourself to achieve so you stay relevant? Again, find someone you admire, study them, and imitate their work ethic.

Personally, I want to write books. Books that help, books that teach, books that entertain and tickle minds.

So what did I do? I took a close look at the two authors whose books I've read more than any others – Stephen King and Anne Rice. I researched them, took a look at their writing habits, and read their thoughts on how they went from zero to hero. And I incorporated their habits into mine. After seeing how much they write and how often they released new books I now write 2,000 words a day and make it my goal to write two books a year, like they do.

I researched what makes an author successful and what publishers look for, and set about creating the sort of platform that would make me stand out. I studied how professional book cover creators incorporated designs and learned how to make covers that popped. And I set about making it easy for people to say "Yes!" when I requested vital retail space to promote my work by being sure I created something yesworthy before even asking.

Want to excel sooner rather than later? Then find what works and copy it. Add your personal flair, but don't bust your head trying to reinvent a winning formula.

Exercise: List one to three relevant role models.

_____

_____

_____

_____

_____

_____

_____

Journal: *Answer these questions:* What traits do you share with your role models? How do they influence you? What do you admire about them? What are they doing that you'll incorporate going forward?

_____

_____

_____

_____

_____

_____

_____

_____

_____

_____

_____

_____

_____

_____

_____

Chapter 12

Define Success In More Ways Than One

This is an especially important rule to remember during the early stages, because it may take a while for the dollars to roll in. If your definition of success only revolves around the amount of money going into your bank account, you might lose hope before your talent gets off the ground.

When I coach women in the relationship of their dreams I teach them early on to take control of their naturally negative brain, so they become more conscious of what's positive. We have a habit of mentally retaining negative occurrences while quickly forgetting positive ones, a throwback to our cavemen brains which helped us survive in the wild. No point making space in our heads for that beautiful sunset when we should be remembering what plant gave us a stomach ache, right?

So, success to me is more than book sales and coaching clients. It's the "Yes" I get for speaking gigs. The women who show up at events saying they feel our encounter is pure fate. The glowing emails I get about the shifts I help people achieve. It's the times my husband shares what he told someone else about my efforts and wins. It's the growing list of followers on my social media platforms and the book selfies fans send me. And it's the laughter, kisses, and relaxed, happy smiles my husband flashes every day because I'm walking my talk.

I take all these little wins and make sure I remember them when nothing seems to be moving forward. I wrap them around me when I feel a little lost and adrift, and remind myself that though one area may seem stagnant I'm still making forward progress *somewhere*.

The fact is you've got to become your biggest motivational guru if you're gonna get yourself going when the going gets tough.

When my business was nothing more than just an idea I attended a retreat that helped women cut through their own bullshit. There, the voice in my head said I should write any compliments I received that weekend, and I did. And thank God too, because for the next year I'd pull that sheet of paper out and remind myself of the things I was losing sight of.

Tucked away in a folder labelled "Personal motivation/inspiration" were the words I needed to remember on this journey.

"You are so healing to me."

"When I saw you I thought, 'Who is this girl?'"

"I gravitate towards you."

"I was impressed by you, and I'm sure there were a few women who were impressed by you. I wish that you could see yourself."

And the most important message of all. "You need to shine."

So I give emotional rewards equal space at the table. My work is all about love, and if I can't love what I do regardless of moulah, I'm putting all my emotional eggs in one basket and there's no balance.

Because of this I feel just as "high" helping someone for free and watching them soar as I do seeing my book sales ramp up and getting deposit notifications from

Amazon. The key is choosing to do something so rewarding that the payoff has multiple streams of income.

What this does is increase your "sustainability" factor. By widening your gaze to include more than one measure of success, you manage to carry your passion through tough times and keep your eye on the ball; your 10 year plan to become an overnight success.

Exercise: List 5 compliments you've received that are relevant to your talent.

_____

_____

_____

_____

_____

Journal: Describe a time where you used your talent and all the ways it rewarded you when you did.

_____

_____

Chapter 13

Don't Let Doubt Overshadow Facts

There are moments when your brain will be your worst enemy. It's common to lose sight of reality and get stuck in a negative mindset, so don't beat yourself up when you're swimming in self-doubt.

The question isn't "Am I right?" when you find yourself there, but rather "What in reality actually counters this train of thought?"

This is why it's important to take stock of all those successes, no matter how small or where they come from. See, doubt is a feeling, and if you've been reading my relationship self-help books you'll know one of my lessons already; not all feelings are true. Sometimes our brain gets tricky and makes stuff up.

So it benefits us to maintain a healthy dose of objective thinking, even about ourselves. Not falling for emotional traps and using our logical minds to analyze ourselves is an extremely useful way to navigate life. And if you can do this, you'll find you can talk yourself out of a lot of negative thought patterns before they take hold and mess things up for you.

So every time you find yourself in a dark mental spin, filled with doubt and a side dish of anguish, stop. I'm serious about that. Stop before that thought goes into autopilot and starts to overshadow everything else. Stop before you start believing the feeling without touching base with reality.

There were times when I wouldn't get a media request for what felt like way too long. I'd find myself wondering if I'd become irrelevant, if my teachings had lost their meaning, if nobody wanted to hear from me after all, and if all this had been a colossal waste of time.

"Stop" I'd tell myself. "When was the last time you were asked to contribute to something bigger than yourself?"

Just a few weeks ago, was the answer.

"Relax then," I'd say to that nagging voice inside my mind. "There will be more, because the best predictor of future behaviour is past behaviour." And then I'd sit and meditate, imagining an editor reaching out to me, and within a few days, voila. "Hey, Chantal! I'm writing an article about …"

Part of the beauty of grounding yourself in reality actually ties into one of the most fundamental laws of nature – like attracts like. If your mind is spinning dark webs of "I'm not good enough, there's no way, I really should just quit because (fill in the blank)" guess what you're attracting?

Failure.

But if you catch yourself and become conscious of what's in your head, you can interject logic into your downward spiral and interrupt the flow of negativity. Which means you'll redirect your thoughts before they become a force that will just pull in more negativity.

So pull your head into Goodness every time you find yourself feeling down. Take out the notes you created when someone acknowledged the good in what you do. Open up your stats and eyeball them again, giving yourself credit for the growth you've created. Remind yourself that your last success wasn't that long ago. Lift yourself back up and enter a mind space where the notion that you are successful reigns. And because like attracts like, your mindset will send out a vibe that will pull in more of what you want instead of leaving you spinning till you keel over from exhaustion.

Exercise: Write your three most common self-negating thoughts. Then write their opposite statement.

_____

_____

_____

_____

_____

_____

Journal: Finish this thought: "I am hard on myself because _____." Then write about why you're more than those thoughts by finishing this statement: "I am accomplished because _____."

_____

_____

_____

Chapter 14

The Universe is Talking to You

I'm the last person to sit here and tell you this journey will be all la-dee-da without times where your head will be up your ass. But those are the very moments the Universe will send you messengers, and it's up to you to pay attention and hear the words they're delivering.

"Ask and you shall receive." Well, sometimes the question spinning inside your head will be, "Am I doing the right thing? Should I continue on? CAN I continue on?!"

I can distinctly remember instances where my dark questions were answered with a resounding "Yes!" by the Universe. This wonderful web of energy that surrounds us all sent me two beautiful messengers to make sure I understood that I was indeed on the right path, and all I needed to do was believe in myself.

"Holy crap. Am I on the right track?" I fearfully asked myself as I stood alone at my second ever trade show moments before the doors opened to let in the crowd. Soon after a young woman rushed to my booth, snatching up my three latest books while passionately exclaiming how much my first one had helped her through the previous year. *Yes, you are*, the Universe was saying.

"Can I keep doing this?" I tiredly asked myself, having just finished setting up for my bazillionth book signing on a tour that would consume almost every weekend that year. "Oh my God, I'm so glad you're here! This is my friend, Susan. Sue, you need this book, and that one. I've got this book, this one, and this one too." *Yes, you must*, said the Universe. *Women need you.*

Listen, it's okay to have doubts now and then. It's completely normal to feel tired, drained, and uninspired from time to time. It's okay to question whether you're on the right path or if you have the energy to sustain your forward momentum. But it's not okay to dismiss the answers you'll get to these questions.

So whip out your pen and paper the moment you get them. Or open up your phone and text yourself the messages you get, and let them sink in. The Universe isn't going to leave you high and dry. Instead, it'll send you what you need when you need it. It's your job to pay attention and give those signals the weight they deserve, because these are the lifelines you'll need when you get tired. Believe the Universe when it wants to help you cross those dark expanses, so you can make it to better times once again.

Exercises: List two or three messages the Universe has sent you about your talent.

_____

_____

_____

_____

_____

_____

_____

Journal: Describe what happened in at least one of those moments. What were you feeling down or confused about? What was the question in your mind? What was the answer, and how was it delivered?

_____

_____

_____

_____

_____

_____

_____

_____

_____

_____

_____

_____

_____

_____

_____

Fear
will not
control me.

Step 3 – Overcoming Fear

Every captain fears the storm, but crosses the ocean regardless

Chapter 16

It's Going to Be Hard

I'm not going to lie to you. There will be tough times as you unfold all the stuff inside your head and heart, and iron out the details until you have a nice, smooth image of what you're building and where you're going.

You will have massive highs. Moments where you can't believe the good fortune that's coming your way. Moments where it seems every door is open and the world is your oyster. Moments where the path to success seems crystal clear and lined with cheerleaders shaking their pop-poms while proud friends and family toss confetti and glitter in the air as you bounce past on a bedazzled Unicorn.

And then, the crash.

Emails will go unanswered. Phone calls unreturned. Doors that seemed wide open now look sealed shut, and you wonder why you're left out in the cold, shivering and hungry because nobody has fed you for what seems like *ever*.

My friend, you are in for one helluva roller coaster ride when you dare step outside your box and open up whole new worlds for yourself. And that's normal. That's why I started this book with meditation. You're going to need the effects meditation can create, now more than ever.

Because the worst case scenario is, instead of moving through difficult emotions like a car cutting through a dense fog, you stay stuck in them for too long. You'll lose your steam if you stall in negative feelings, compounded by a lack of forward momentum, and let all that make you think this current moment is the status quo.

It's not. Not if you do two things, non-stop, regardless of what's happening around you. Constant forward movement, no matter how small, and meditation.

Have you ever watched a documentary about people ascending Mount Everest or read a book written by one of those crazy-brave folks? I have, and two things stood out the most. One was learning a new phrase, *digital extraction* (I'll let your imagination run with that. Thankfully, it's irrelevant here). But the second thing I learned by studying those who put themselves through one of the most grueling experiences on earth is this: when it comes to reaching a goal there comes a time when all you need to focus on is putting one foot in front of the other.

Look, you know as well as I do that the biggest reward comes after the biggest challenge. Having a baby, buying a house, getting that job, travelling throughout the world, all those came with a hefty price on your body and your time, and arrived after years of devotion to a cause.

Don't expect this to be any different.

I've said it before: there are a lot of starters but not a lot of finishers. I've personally seen many people fall off the road to success, then just stay on the ground moaning their distress while the rest of us plowed on, too intent on our destination to give in to hunger and fatigue.

Only those of us who dig deep will find strength beyond what our last meal gave us, beyond the rest our last sleep offered, and keep our eyes on lifting our boots and placing them down, one after another. We are the ones who will cross the finish line. We are the few who will ascend that mountain.

Know that when all of your body's resources are depleted it's your brain that'll give you the energy needed to keep going. The willpower to get through those hard moments and taste the success your constant forward motion will give you will depend on what you allow inside your own mind.

Do you think anyone who got to the top of Mount Everest and lived to tell the tale ever doubted themselves? Sure. But did they let that doubt guide their actions? Most definitely not, and the proof is in the pudding. They got to the top.

Your brain is your greatest tool. Use it right, and you've got a chance.

Exercise: Create a mantra that will help uplift you through tough moments.

_____

_____

_____

_____

_____

Journal: Write about the last big hurdle you got through. Describe how you felt at the lowest low, how you found your way up and out, and how you felt when it was resolved.

_____

_____

_____

_____

_____

_____

_____

_____

_____

_____

_____

_____

_____

_____

Chapter 17

Is It Plugged In?

Make no mistake: though we divorced, my first husband is awesomeness wrapped in awesomesauce. He taught me a lot about great feelings like safety, security, and confidence, and showed me how to look at situations with a level head.

Back then he was in charge of maintenance at his company, and I'll never forget the question he answered first whenever a problem cropped up.

Is it plugged in?

Let me bring you back to that famous quote by dear William of Ockham again, "All things being equal, the simplest solution tends to be the best one."

When I work with clients it's common for me to help them through what I call "kitty in a tree" moments. Those are the times when their minds start to whirl, and though they managed to confidently climb to those far up branches and gain a better vantage point on their lives, they suddenly find themselves distracted by the distance to the ground and panic sets in.

I'll get a frantic message about how their minds are spinning so much they can't see their way out of the mental spiral they're tumbling down, and I calmly walk them through my *is it plugged in* checklist.

Below are the questions I ask, essentially directing them to get down on all fours and make sure the plug didn't fall out of the outlet. Which, to be honest, is usually the case:

Are you meditating?

Have you gone for a walk?

Are you eating well?

Do you need to fix a fight you're having with someone?

This list represents the basics when it comes to your well-being. If these have been neglected, guess what? You've come unplugged in one form or another, and the lack of juice is wreaking havoc on your ability to function effectively.

Now, I'm not unreasonable, and experience has shown me it takes a few turns around the block before you'll remember to check the plug first and foremost. These repeatable instructions will help you come back up whenever you're sinking into darkness, so fold the corner of this page over because you'll come back to it time and again.

First, catch yourself. Don't let your feelings run unchecked because that's when you get into trouble. Until you rewire your brain and become a better functioning machine you're still operating on old programming. That's why it's important to get good at realizing your mind is off and running down the wrong corridor, then redirecting it towards where you actually want it to go.

So if you're feeling off emotionally, stop. Just literally stop what you're doing. Stop walking, stop reading, stop doing, and take stock of your brain. It's yours to control, so go right ahead and do that. It's a habit that needs to be formed, and there's no time like the present.

Second, ask yourself if you're still plugged in. If it's been three days or more since you last meditated, then that's your first step. Hell, if it's been one day this is still your first step! Because if you're spinning in negativity, you'll benefit from shrinking your amygdala and reducing your bodily stress responses. Meditation will lower the amount of cortisol coursing through your body and help you feel more relaxed, and a more relaxed *you* is better equipped to make the right decisions.

So grab your headphones, go to a quiet spot, and spend at least 10 minutes calming your brain.

Third, get yourself moving forward physically. Long before I was a people whisperer I was a dog whisperer, and one thing a good trainer understands is, if the brain is spinning the body needs to get moving.

My specialty back then was behaviour modification, or dogs who were "problems" to their owners. And like a good trainer, I always taught dog daddies and mammas to get walking instead of staying stuck in a dysfunctional moment. Your dog is overly excited? Get walking. It's trying to eat that other dog and barking frantically? Get walking. It's trying to shrink itself into the sidewalk in fear? Get walking.

Because physically moving one's body helps the brain unlock from the current situation. It's hard to stay stuck mentally when the body is in motion, because your brain and body are constantly feeding information back and forth. So if your brain is feeding stress responses to your body, go ahead and help reverse that by sending movement signals up to the brain instead.

Listen, thinking you are beyond your own control is how you're going to end up out of control. But taking control of yourself means you're going to get better and better at managing what's happening inside you. You've got the power, Dear Reader, so don't be afraid to exercise it.

And finally, if what's preoccupying you is something you need to fix in your relationships, then do it. Avoidance will only get you so far, but ensuring you have a rock steady base of operations, meaning your home space and heart space, means you've added superpowers to your toolkit.

If this is something you need help with, I've got you covered. Wherever you're at in your love life, check out my books and read the one that's right for you. Then apply the steps I've laid out and watch your world change for the better. Because ultimately the amount of peaceful love you have – or the amount of combative love you're experiencing – will taint everything you do. So be sure you're spreading good vibes into your work, 'cause what goes around really does come around.

Exercise: Write your "Is it plugged in?" checklist. Put it on the fridge.

_____

_____

_____

_____

_____

Journal: Write a scenario when you don't feel any stress. Describe the situation/scene in detail. Where are you? What's happening? How are you feeling? Then take a moment to truly savor the memory, and let it become part of your emotional world again.

_____

_____

_____

_____

_____

_____

_____

Chapter 18

Be Okay With Change

If you don't think evolution is part of your business model, then you've got no business starting a business.

There is nothing in this world that is inflexible and unchanging, and if you're coming into a business with that sort of mentality, you're setting yourself up for failure. Because unless you can follow the laws of nature, meaning you're able to shift and evolve along with the rest of your environment, you're going to be left sitting in your ideas while the rest of the world moves on.

Your fourth photo shoot, whether it's of you or your product, will look different from your first one. Your sales model might change along with shifts in online marketing tools. And your business vision should change and adjust over time too, because you're meditating and tapping into the deepest parts of your inner light.

And sometimes change can seem scary. It might mean dropping something you always thought was going to be a part of your plan. It might mean doing something you've never done before. It might mean doubling your workload to accommodate new dreams and new directions popping up in your mind.

And the biggest change of all could be a change in lifestyle as you lean more into your passion. You might have less money to do those fun things you used to enjoy so much. Less time to see friends and family. Less energy to dispense overall, because you're going through moments of absolute consumption with your work.

And all that is okay.

Listen, the less rigid you are going into this, the more likely it is you'll turn your inner heart's desire into something fulfilling on multiple levels. You need to be able to flow from one thought to another, from one experiment to another, and from one situation to another without losing your shit because "this isn't what I thought was going to happen". And if you can be this fluid, you'll be practising Mother Nature's number one law of survival – adaptability.

If the lizards on the Galapagos Islands hadn't developed the ability to dive underwater and find food sources there, they wouldn't be there today. So be a Galapagos lizard and learn how to roll with Mamma Nature. You'll end up outlasting those who decide to stay stuck in their ways.

Exercise: Practice releasing negative emotions as they happen. Start becoming comfortable feeling uncomfortable. List negative feelings you want to release.

_____

_____

_____

_____

_____

Journal: Describe a past situation when you thought an impending change would suck but then realized that the change was actually for the better. What was the situation? What changed? How did that change create positive improvements in your life?

_____

_____

_____

_____

_____

_____

_____

_____

_____

_____

_____

_____

_____

_____

_____

Chapter 19

Be Okay With Taking Breaks

If you've noticed the dates of publications on my books, you'll realize I've had some pretty crazy work schedules. But interspersed throughout the intense building phases of my early years were breaks that helped me relax and regroup. In fact, the longest and most relaxing one I've taken in the past three years happened just before I started writing this book.

Studies have shown that vacations are very much needed, and those who take them tend to come back to work with a higher degree of productivity. But our cultural go-go-go mentality can make us feel guilty for even thinking about taking those breaks.

And to that I say, "Quit that shit."

Listen, guilt under most circumstances is a very normal human emotion. But our mistake is taking that feeling and letting it direct our behaviours more often than it should. (Side note: If you're a woman, you're likely to feel guilt more often and more intensely than men. It's an ingrained emotional response intent of making you a better mother. Just sayin'.)

Your brain will need a rest every now and then. But taking that break and making yourself feel bad about it is counter-productive, like drinking a big cup of coffee and a Coke right before bed. Sure, your thirst is quenched when you lie down, but you're not going to get the restorative sleep you actually need.

So give yourself a break when you need it or when you're between massive projects. Your energy, like everything on this planet, has fluctuations. Personally, I compare my own energy outputs to waves lapping on a shore. Sometimes they come up high, with plenty of force behind them. Sometimes they rock gently back and forth. But my energy is always in motion and always shifting, anywhere from intense to barely moving.

Accept your rhythms, and give yourself permission to go with the flow.

Exercise: List three things that help you unwind and relax.

_____

_____

_____

_____

_____

Journal: Describe a scene where you are perfectly relaxed. Write it in detail. Where are you? What are you doing? What are the sights and smells? Describe the sensations in your body. Then, let yourself bask in the notion of feeling completely at peace.

_____

_____

_____

_____

_____

_____

_____

_____

Chapter 20

Be Okay With F*ck Ups

I stood frozen in front of about 30 women, microphone in hand, while I stared at the empty space between the tip of the stage and the first row of seats. Silence hung in the air between us as I searched for the next sentence, and the audience waited for me to begin speaking again.

I was blank.

It was the first time I'd given that particular talk, and in my over-confidence I had failed to make notes to bring on stage. Only days before I'd hastily whipped together the Power Point presentation, but as I stared at the next slide my brain failed to remember the lesson associated to the words on screen.

Tick. Tock. The moment dragged into eternity as it stretched outside the realms of simple pause into obvious dysfunction.

I waited. And so did they.

After what was obviously too long my mind flooded with words again, and I was off. But not soon enough, and I watched as half my audience got up and left.

I wrapped up my talk and walked back to my trade show booth.

"How did it go?" asked Kim, my assistant.

"It went really well!" I exclaimed, intent on not letting this mistake ruin my vibe.

If there was one thing I understood about human nature, it was that confidence breeds confidence just as surely as a bad mood repels anyone who came close.

"Alright! Let's sell some books!" I said, smiling as I gave Kim a hug to warm her soul and give us both a boost of positive energy. "We've got some women who need us!"

The next day I told her about my lapse on stage. We were talking about confidence and the importance of not letting circumstances shake our own self-belief.

"Did you know I totally blanked out during my first talk yesterday?" I asked, and her eyes grew wide. "Nooooooo!" she said, shocked. "What happened?!"

"Well, I totally forgot what I wanted to say and just stood there." I laughed. "But you wouldn't have known it when I came back, right?"

"No!" she exclaimed. "I had no idea!"

"And that's because I wasn't going to let it affect me. It was a moment, and that was all. But I wasn't going to let that moment change how I felt, and I wasn't going to let it influence my ability to talk to women and sell books. I wasn't going to let it bring me down, take away my confidence, or make me upset. Because we're infecting each other all the time, and the last thing I want to do is infect people with negative energy. So I just let it pass without making it something that would last longer than it needed to. It happened, and I let it stay in the past once I was through it."

See, when it comes to life you've got to be capable of developing a strong mental "Fuck it" tool to use in those moments where you're at a crossroads. Either beat yourself up for a mistake, letting your mind twist and turn and roll it over and over, vomiting the memory and associated uncomfortable feelings into your present on an endless loop.

Or.

Say fuck it. It happened, and I'll take steps to avoid that particular error from happening again (You bet I had notes on the podium when I gave that talk again the next morning).

Life is not without mistakes, and most of them you can just let slide on by without making an emotional fuss. Making a wrong turn, searching the wrong aisle, calling someone by the wrong name. These are all small mistakes that we turn into simple lessons and move past without overthinking.

So what I want you to do is take that same mindset and apply it to your bigger mistakes.

Listen, there's nothing wrong with regret. In fact it's one of life's biggest emotional lessons. I often tell people that I love regret, because it's the feeling that keeps me from repeating the kind of mistakes that should never be done twice.

Like when I was in my mid 20s and had two situations collide into a massive nuclear clusterfuck. A roommate's abusive boyfriend and my own low self-esteem imploded when I pushed for adherence to our agreement about letting others move into the apartment. His anger at my refusal to accept him and aggression towards women culminated in him pushing me onto my bed and smacking me in the face.

Stunned, I shut my bedroom door and called a friend crying. And that was all I did.

I soon moved out, but for years afterwards my stomach would literally twist while guttural sounds of anxiety escaped my throat every time that moment came to mind. Until I elevated my esteem enough to stop letting people push me around, I was tortured by the thought that I had actually let that happen.

Never again, I told myself over and over. *Never again.*

And over time, drawing on that white hot tortured regret, I slowly built myself up. *I don't ever want to feel that way inside my body. Not for years like that. Not for one more minute.*

I used that intense, lingering pain to form my actions. My question when I arrived at a crossroad where the choice was to step down from what I really wanted or stand up for myself was, "Do I want to live with the feeling of regret for years to come?"

And the answer was always a resounding NO.

It takes courage to avoid regret. That's the beauty of choosing actions that don't pull you into negative emotions. It's either be brave or live with a stomach full of knots each time you remember when you didn't insist on what was right for you.

I don't regret blanking out on a stage in front of dozens of women, because I was brave enough to get back on that horse and do a better job the next time around.

And though I hate that moment where I was pushed down and hit, it was most definitely the last time someone put their hands on me. I learned to disallow disrespect. I learned to shake off negative feelings by asking myself what was the lesson I needed to take forward. And I learned to intervene on my own behalf, before making more decisions I'd regret down the road.

I learned from my mistakes and gave myself permission to make them. Because life isn't perfect. You're going to make mistakes, but your emotional wellbeing and future hutzpah depends on you being able to step back, assess the situation, take the lesson, shake it all off, and move forward with enough confidence to do better.

Dragging your regret behind you like a wagon full of steaming poo doesn't help you one bit, and it certainly won't help your business. Again, we're infecting each other at all times with our inner vibe, so even if you're masking your feelings with a smile, you're still stinking on a subconscious level.

And people will be wrinkling their noses and walking away from you, not fully understanding why they feel a measure of repulsion but acting on it anyway.

Lose, lose.

Maybe I blanked out on stage so I could see how easily I recovered from worst case scenarios. Maybe it happened so Kim could see how something viewed as disastrous could be left behind the moment it was done. I know we both learned something from that story.

Because ultimately, it's not the situations in life that form you, it's how you deal with them after the fact that will have the most profound effects.

A while back I was doing some research into how to effectively deal with post-traumatic stress disorder. Now fair warning, I'm about to be pretty vague here, because I don't remember the title of the book and I'm working from nothing more than a lingering memory, but something stood out at the time.

Those who had an emotional breakdown immediately after the traumatic situation were more likely to suffer from post-traumatic symptoms, compared to those who managed to quickly regain their emotional marbles and move forward.

Every moment in life will carve itself into your brain. The question is, how deep will it cut? When something disastrous happens grab that situation by the shoulders and say, "Not today!" while giving it a shake so it's fruits fall at your feet. Then, pick those nuggets of Goodness up, wipe the dirt off of them, and take big, nourishing bites of lifelong lessons that help make you a bigger, better, stronger, more resilient human being.

Because ultimately, that's what those are all about. Tests to your resilience, strength, and staying power. Will you pass? Or will you fail? The choice is up to you, and that choice takes place moment by moment.

Use regret to culminate more of what you need. More preparation. More insight. More confidence. More bounce. It's only bad when you don't give yourself the focus you need to make a powerful comeback.

Exercise: List two to three things you regret and now use as a lesson.

_____

_____

_____

_____

_____

Journal: Make a promise to yourself to never allow regret to hold you back by describing what you'll do when faced with mistakes.

_____

_____

_____

_____

_____

_____

_____

_____

Chapter 21

Switch the Script Inside Your Head

Admit it – there's a voice yammering away inside your mind. You call it your own and take its message to heart without question.

"Ugh. I look terrible."

"What are you thinking? You can't do this."

"I'm not worthy."

What if I told you that sometimes the voice inside your head isn't actually you? What if that nagging voice of doubt and negativity is nothing more than ghosts from your past, fading in every so often to haunt you?

That voice is called *conditioning*.

Conditioning is sometimes the most damaging aspect of our lives. And though this twisting, slimy, slithering, wormlike creature wasn't born from your belly, it still attaches itself to your boob, sucking the life out of you bit by bit.

Yuck.

It's time to unlatch that sucker and toss it aside, to wither and die from lack of nourishment.

It's unfortunate that there were sources in your life that vomited insecurities into you. They taught you that feeling good about yourself is harder than it should be. They made you feel that what was good was *maybe* attainable, but what was awesome was likely out of reach. Maybe it was a family member, or maybe it was the media's message that perfection is something far different from what you are. Whatever the source of that nagging, negative voice in your head, it's time to divert your attention from it and bring your focus into the here and now.

And as with everything that ends with success, you've got to start with a plan. That means pinpointing the negative messaging so you can come up with an opposite statement. You then have your mantra for moments where you realize there's something unhealthy happening inside your head. Remember, catch yourself a million times a day!

"Ugh. I look terrible" should be interrupted and replaced with "I look good enough!"

"What are you thinking? You can't do this" can be replaced with "I've got this. I'm smart enough, hardworking enough, and I've got the motivation to become better at my talent while growing it into something meaningful."

"I'm not worthy" should most definitely be interrupted every time and replaced with "I deserve love and recognition for my efforts."

Redirecting is another one of those "until" tactics. Until you switch that negative inner dialogue to something that feels good and motivating, your work isn't done. And until you stop unrealistically viewing yourself, you've got to keep working at switching that dialogue.

I use the word *realistic* here because I'm the last person to blow bubbles up your butt, and I don't want to encourage you to do that either. You do need to avoid over-inflating your efforts, because doing so would get in the way of your potential for real success.

Listen, if you're putting in zero time in voice training, it's not realistic to tell yourself you'll be the next winner on The Voice. But if you're putting in the time and training and are seeing improvements, you need to give yourself credit for growth towards your potential. *I'm hard working, and with this work ethic I'll achieve success.*

I'm not like everyone else, and I don't need to be. I can be appreciated for my individuality and how that translates into my talent and passion.

I'm constantly checking in on myself, asking how I feel and what's inside my mind. If there's negativity, my next question is, is this valid? Maybe I feel stagnant, because for the past week I haven't buckled down or I'm feeling overwhelmed and flighty. Which means my course of action is making a checklist of my next four steps, and getting them done to put myself back on track.

But maybe it's just a nagging voice of doubt tugging at me despite my efforts and the wins that materialized from them pulling me down into a space I really don't belong in. And that requires an intervention on my part. A redirect to what I should be thinking instead.

"You're losing your touch. Nobody is reaching out and asking to publish your advice." *No, that's not true. I've had three major news articles quote me in the past month. My advice is valid and sought out, and my work is paying off into recognition on a national level.*

"Your books are no good. Nobody wants to read them." *No, that's not true. I've received multiple emails in the past week from women who have reached out to let me know how I've helped them. Women also say they read my books more than once and lend them out to friends. I am a good writer, and my content is enjoyed and utilized in amazing ways.*

You see, your mind is yours and yours only. Sure, some nasty stuff might have been planted there when you weren't looking, slipping through and wriggling its way inside your head. But intervention is not beyond your control, and the words that should never escape your lips are, "I can't help it."

Because yes, you can.

Look, the kind of thinking that shouldn't cross your mind will likely happen. I say that because even though I've gained enough street cred to write for our country's biggest news sources, even though my books are literally selling themselves online, even though women gush about how much their thinking has changed about love and self-love when they see me, and even though I've been meditating for three years straight and have shrunk my amygdala considerably, I still have moments where I have to push self-negating thoughts out of my brain.

And I'm starting to think this is part of the price to pay for being human.

So when those thoughts come up, go easy on yourself. Catch yourself having them instead of allowing your emotions to fall in step. Tap into reality, whatever that may be, and redirect your train of thought.

Exercise: Create the uplifting mantra you'll use when your mind is overtaken by self-negating thoughts.

_____

_____

_____

_____

_____

_____

_____

_____

Journal: Write about a time when you realized a thought you had about yourself was actually wrong. What was the thought? What turned your impression around? How did you feel when that happened?

_____

_____

_____

_____

_____

_____

_____

_____

_____

_____

_____

_____

_____

_____

Chapter 22

Manage Your Expectations

I've written six books on love now, and one of the most important lessons I teach is to work hard, then release the outcome.

Nothing kills love more than frustrating yourself with a story inside your head. Giving with one hand while holding out the other for immediate payback is how you'll nix that beautiful sense of gratitude from which love freely flows. It's also how you'll end up warping your own mind with feelings of dissatisfaction and frustration.

Lose, lose.

When it comes to love, the best feeling is one that looks like this: "Wow! My partner is sooooo awesome; what can I do to make them feel as great as I do?"

But this doesn't happen when each gift is laden with expectations. *You better get on that payback lickety split; otherwise, there's gonna be a fight a-brewin'.* That sort of giving never actually feels like a gift for either party.

Conversely, finding joy in giving for the sake of giving means your offers come with a happy heart. And since we're always infecting each other, the receiver senses the purity of your actions and feels good being a beneficiary. And this is where awesome Goodness happens in relationships, building higher and higher as giving is shifted back and forth and appreciation for each other increases. See? Mmmmmmmagic.

So what does this have to do with building your passion into something significant? Well, it's the same idea. If you've got an inflexible expectation in mind when you start doling out your hard work, thinking it has to pay off or generate a number of followers within a certain amount of time, chances are if those deadlines are missed, you'll start to lose some of your motivation to keep plugging away.

And that, my Dear Reader, will be the beginning of the end of your odyssey.

Your passion will be dampened by disappointment, your zest and fire cooled by thoughts like "Maybe what I want to do ain't all that." Doubt can creep in, and you'll start to question whether you should even be trying.

Ugh.

But those thoughts are literally *you* getting in your own way by trying to read how the future should pan out. It's kind of like looking into the future expecting a fire to continue burning bright while presently neglecting to put another piece of wood on the flames.

Listen, expectations reside in the future, don't they? But you, and everything that's within your control, is right here in the present. And if you keep plugging away in the present moment, your future will unfold much better than if you kept missing expected marks and losing motivation.

So it's okay to have goals. It's okay to create a business plan and to have forward thinking statements. But it's not okay to let expectations eat away at what you could ultimately accomplish because you let them bring you down.

And remember, everything you have will be a product of your unrelenting drive to pour your heart into something that lights you up. Just don't let your head get in your way.

Exercise: List what you love to give and don't care about receiving payback for.

_____

_____

_____

_____

_____

Journal: Describe a moment in your life when giving felt better than receiving. What did you do? Who was the beneficiary? How did you feel about giving that gift? How did they feel about receiving it?

_____

_____

_____

_____

_____

_____

_____

_____

Chapter 23

Are You Sure?

The Universe is a fickle lover. She wants reassurances, and will absolutely test your resolve. How? By raising a hand and stopping you dead in your tracks, so she can look you square in the eye and ask the most important question of all.

Are you sure?

Because she doesn't want to waste her time. She's got standards, you know. She's not just letting any schmo come through her door and take up her energy. She's going to put you through the grinder and make sure you're committed.

Before I pour more of myself into you, I need to know. Are you sure?

Just when things seem to be heating up you're likely going to hit a roadblock. I say likely because I've never seen someone *not* hit one when they're going through this journey of self-evolution, but I don't want to speak in absolutes either.

But if you're prepared to feel like a stick suddenly got jammed into the spokes of your bicycle, you'll have some hindsight to help you through that sticky moment.

I'll tell you a story that helps highlight this type of occurrence.

One of my best and brightest students, let's call her Lucy, came to me a year and a half ago in a state of near panic. She was in a downward spiral triggered by a horrendous break up, and despite her efforts to find her way out the ongoing feelings of helplessness, it left her feeling suicidal.

Lucy was desperate for a change and made the decision to lean into my teachings and follow my advice to the letter.

I taught her how to meditate and re-direct her thoughts, and she worked at shrinking the part of her brain that was contributing to her negative emotions. I helped her clarify who she was so she could boost her self-esteem, and got her on a path of self-care. And I helped her through her "kitty in a tree" moments, when all the things I taught her flew out the window because negative loops came cycling back.

Slowly but surely, with consistent work and focus in the right direction, Lucy began to change her brain, and her emotional world started to shift. She started to have more up moments than down and to savour life again. She discovered joy that had been long buried and took more control of her interactions as her self-esteem rose and she became more protective of her energy.

She started standing up for herself and became stronger and stronger within her heart and mind. Then, Lucy started to feel...Happy.

And that was when the Universe stepped forward and asked her, "Are you sure?"

A long buried incident came to light, and Lucy was asked to testify in court. The thought of facing someone who had massively contributed to her misery terrified her, and she took an emotional nosedive as the memories came flooding back, this time with a vengeance. She could no longer run away from her past, and Lucy had to double down to work through this next leg of her difficult journey.

"I don't know what to do" she said to me, near tears. "I can't sleep, and I feel so stressed out all the time."

I directed her to increase her meditation minutes, prescribing specific tracks on my Let's Meditate playlist on You Tube that would help calm her post traumatic stress. I gave her new mantras and helped her find redirects to counter this fresh batch of negative thoughts. And I reminded her to make sure she was plugged in, walking her through her checklist of easy solutions to ensure she was maximizing on self-care.

And Lucy pulled through this next phase of difficulty with flying colours. Her answer to the Universe? *Yes, yes, I am ready. And thank you for the test, because now I feel even stronger than before. Now I know I'm ready for anything.*

I gotta admit, I just teared up here. It's such a beautiful thing when the Universe puts you to the test, because when you pass you end up levelling up in your journey. You hit new heights, and you prove to yourself just how strong, capable, and emotionally intelligent you've become. Your resistance gets a boost, and your self-esteem rises above the crap this world will toss your way.

In essence, you develop super-powers.

The Universe doesn't test you, asking "are you sure" to bring you down. It does so because it recognizes the trajectory you've chosen and supports it 100%. But you know as well as I do, growth comes from a certain measure of painful effort.

You don't get strong muscles at the gym without days where you're wincing every time you get out of the car. You don't get that degree without nights where you've crammed so hard for an exam your head hurts. And you don't become an emotional leader and a business ninja without days where you've had to rebuild the mental house you so carefully constructed.

Such is life. Growing pains always accompany growth, and the sooner you absorb this truth the better prepared you'll be when the Universe smacks you with a stinging blow.

Are you sure? Yes, Universe. Yes, I am.

Exercise: List three moments in your life when you didn't let fear get in your way.

_____

_____

_____

_____

_____

_____

Journal: Describe a moment when you overcame something and became a stronger person because of it. What obstacle were you facing? How did you overcome it? How did you feel afterwards? What is the lifelong lesson you take away from that experience?

_____

_____

_____

_____

_____

_____

_____

_____

_____

_____

_____

Chapter 24

Everything is Going to be Okay

I searched frantically for the next exit, hoping I'd be able to pull off the busy highway before I passed out behind the wheel of my car and caused a deadly accident.

My heart pounded in my chest and it seemed like no matter how much I breathed, oxygen just wasn't getting into my system. My throbbing brain felt like it wanted to spill out of my skull, and I could feel darkness creeping in from the periphery of my eyesight, trying to take over my world. Numbness, emanating from my neck, slowly crept down my arms, and I lowered my chin and put all my focus into staying in my lane.

I was having a panic attack.

It wasn't the first one I'd experienced on my way to a gig. I'd had to pull over once before as those same symptoms overtook my body. I'd never experienced anything like that prior to starting my business journey, but I knew one thing for sure.

It wasn't going to stop me.

For the second time I eased my way to the next exit and parked my car with a sigh of relief. I shakily uncorked my water bottle, taking a few sips before stepping out and forcing myself to walk on wobbly legs until I felt my strength come back.

I am strong. I am powerful. I am in control, I whispered to myself over and over, working double time to infuse my mind with a mantra that would counter the panic wrapping itself around my heart.

I breathed deep to four counts, taking a page from Navy Seals to counter the physiological responses to the stress I was feeling. After a few minutes the pounding in my chest subsided, my strength flowed back, and my mind calmed.

Everything is going to be okay.

I'll be honest, I'm the last person I thought would ever suffer a panic attack. When the first one struck I wasn't even sure what was going on, initially wondering if some sort of medical crisis was taking place.

And it wasn't like the events I was on my way to were beyond anything I'd ever done before. I had already spoken in front of crowds and I'd already done numerous book signings, so why the sudden physical and emotional takedown?

I didn't know.

But I wasn't going to let that direct my course of actions. So instead of turning my car around, I checked to see if I was still plugged in. I soothed myself back to calmness, took a walk to move myself forward, and ensured I was filling my mind with the words I needed instead of letting myself become overwhelmed with the emotions I was experiencing. And like the hero I'd become, I threw my cape back on and took off once again.

Everything is going to be okay.

Look, you're going to face some major emotional hurdles. Between the Universe putting a spoke in your wheels to make you face your resolve, to moments of sheer panic *just because*, you may be in for a wild stomach churning ride from time to time.

And that's okay, because you're going to be fine as long as you realize two things. One, that your body is yours to control, and if you take steps to do so the moment will pass and you'll likely hit a new level of resilience. And two, that a moment is just that − a moment. Reminding yourself that everything is always moving means you'll remember this won't last forever, and with the right steps you'll be okay.

When you're pounding out your passion, putting your all into birthing talent into this world, you're bound to face some pretty intense feelings. Nervousness, anxiety, fear, stress, and maybe even panic will rear up from time to time. Don't turn away when this happens. Instead, face it head on and get yourself through the moment. You'll learn, like I did, that everything is going to be okay.

Exercise: List what you do (or can do) to talk yourself through emotionally tough moments.

_____

_____

_____

_____

_____

_____

Journal: Write about one of the most trying times in your life and how you got through it. What was happening? How were you feeling? What were the steps you took to work through it? How did you feel after it was over? What was the lesson you pulled from that experience?

_____

_____

_____

_____

_____

_____

_____

_____

_____

_____

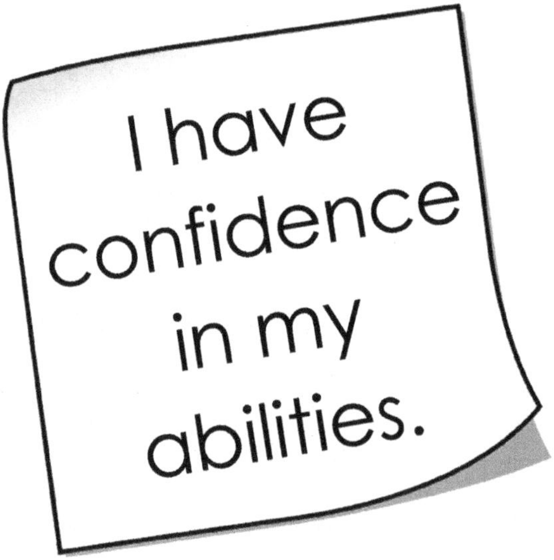
I have
confidence
in my
abilities.

Step 4 – Connect

A labour of love is always born from great enthusiasm and energy.

Chapter 25

How to Brand Yourself

As you step out into this world, carrying your talent like a newborn baby in your arms and proudly showing it to everyone around, one of the things you'll be delving into is how to brand yourself.

Human beings are conscious machines carrying around subconscious reasonings and reactions, and you're often reading this world on a level that's functioning far below your awareness. Hence the term, knee jerk reaction. You're thinking things before you even know you're thinking them.

This is why branding plays such a crucial role in your business model. Branding is, in essence, how you'll trigger people's first impression of what you offer. And if you don't properly convey yourself within the first seven seconds, you're missing valuable opportunities.

Now, I'm not claiming to be a business and marketing strategic dynamo here. But I've done my share of research, something I invite you to do too by the way, and discovered aspects of branding that have an immediate effect on how people subconsciously perceive you.

Let me bring your attention to the use of colour. First, take a look at TV commercials and pay special attention to the colours of inconsequential background props, like that vase on a shelf and the clothes actors are wearing. If you haven't noticed yet, they're usually the same colour scheme as the product being sold to you. Coincidence? Nope.

Marketing agencies know you'll subconsciously pick up on that colour being flashed before your eyes. They're hoping to imprint it into your brain, so you're more likely to recognize that bottle on the shelf when you hit the grocery store.

They also know that certain colours will leave specific emotional aftertastes inside you. It's no mistake that companies that want you to trust what they say use blue, the colour of communication. Or that those who want you to think they're eco-friendly use green, the colour of nature. And if they want you to connect them to love they'll infuse their product with pink, the colour of unconditional love. Ahem.

And I like to add turquoise to my branding because it's the colour of introspection and communication, two vital aspects I teach that facilitate our journey towards love.

So as you're stitching your business together and thinking of how you'll formulate your logo and build your website, designs from which you'll create business cards and promo material, ask yourself, "What sort of *feeling* do I want my customers to have? What do I want them to *think* when they look at me and my products?" Then, research what colours leave those impressions and make them the foundation of your branding.

Listen, the wheel has already been invented here. If you want to market yourself in an effective way, then isn't studying big brands and how they advertise the smartest thing to do? They've already paid a bazillion dollars to be educated on how to trigger our buying choices, so we might as well learn from them.

Another thing to consider when you're putting together your visual impact is your business name. Again, it's all about the thoughts and feelings they'll get with that first impression. You want to communicate clarity about your business because that gives your customer a sense of your surety, and you also want to add a message that leaves them feeling confident in your capabilities.

Maybe your business is making rhinestone pasties, so you might go with Sparkle Tattas and use colours like red to induce excitement.

You might want to sell your beautiful handmade afghan blankets on Etsy and call your business Nicky's Cozy Corner while using pale greens to convey stress reduction and comfort.

Maybe you're coming out as a business consultant, naming your business Shazam and branding yourself with strong blues to let people know they can count on your verbal expertise.

Whatever your choice of words or colour, the impact is immediate, so it's up to you to choose your messaging wisely.

Exercise: List the thoughts and feelings you want your potential customer to experience when they come across your business. Then, write what colours will match them.

_____

_____

_____

_____

_____

_____

_____

Journal: _Answer these questions:_ What is your favourite colour? How does it make you feel?

_____

_____

_____

_____

_____

_____

_____

_____

Chapter 26

Don't Be a Shrinking Violet

You, my dear, are one in a million. That means in a global population of approximately 7.5 billion, there are currently thousands of other humans on this planet who are just like you. My point is, you'll get lost in the crowd if you don't dare to be bold.

One of the most important lessons I've learned has been to let myself *shine*. It was a message the Universe sent my way multiple times, from a new friend putting a sparkly bracelet on my wrist insisting I push myself to "shine as much on the outside as you do on the inside" to having the word "shine, shine, shine" chanted into my ear at a women's retreat because "that's the message for you."

It was a transformational message, and one that I certainly did need. You see, I'd spent much of my early life being quite the wallflower, shrinking away from attention more often than not. It was a defensive measure, something I was doing to avoid the subconscious backlash I received when I got more attention than the girl beside me.

But the Universe had other plans, and part of that plan involved allowing myself to be noticed above the crowd. And if that was going to happen, I needed to shine, and shine bright. And so messengers came and let me know that now was the time to push myself into the spotlight.

And the fact is, if you work with a marketing expert, they'll say the same thing. "If you want to be noticed, you've got to be ahead of the crowd." But in order to be noticed you have to not be afraid to be noticed. And that can mean stepping outside your box so you can step into the ring, where you'll try to beat out your other contenders by outglowing them.

What if your business is multi-level marketing, and numerous people in your region are selling the same brand of lipstick, essential oils, or diet products? If you can't be different, you'll get lost in the multitude of

Facebook posts gushing about how effective that particular item is.

That means you've got to dig deep and uncover that quality about yourself that makes you, personally, more appealing than the rest. Maybe it's your zany sense of humour woven into your live videos. Maybe it's your deep sense of empathy and compassion tied into the benefits of what you offer.

Whatever it is, find it and double down on that quality. Draw it out, magnify it, and rub that all over what you do. I might be a one in a million Dating & Relationship Coach, but what differentiates me is my passion for words and teaching, combined with my own life experiences. So not only have I written several books on the topic of love, but I've woven my story into them, inviting people to glimpse how I've used the sciences I describe to fix my own shortcomings.

Listen, usually you can't tuck yourself into a safe corner while trying to drum up enough interest in your purpose to make it successful. I'm not saying it's impossible, but this sort of tactic creates a greater uphill battle than stepping out of your comfort zone and pushing yourself into people's line of sight.

And people are like crows, drawn to bright, dazzling objects. And like crows, we also tend to pick up those objects and take them home so we can continue to admire them. So be that sparkly thing in the grass. Step far outside of your box if need be. Encourage your potential customers to pick you out of a crowd and see you as unique, special, and exuding a star quality that both warms and lights them up.

Exercise: What personal qualities make you stand out?

_____

_____

_____

_____

_____

Journal: Describe a time when you felt like you stood out in the crowd. Where were you? What were you doing? How did it feel? Then take a moment to bask in those feelings again.

_____

_____

_____

Chapter 27

Become a Public Relations Pro

Very few people are going to know about you if you don't know how to talk yourself up.

One of the first things you should learn is how to condense your message into what's called an "elevator pitch": the premise of a super short pitch that easily conveys what you're all about comes from an imagined scenario, one where you find yourself in an elevator with someone who can massively advance your career in one fell swoop.

You're a crafter who's in the elevator with Martha Stewart. You're a screenwriter in the elevator with Steven Spielberg. You're a dog trainer in the elevator with Caesar Milan. You've got 30 seconds to impress the pants off of them before those gleaming doors open and they step onto their floor and out of your life.

Go!

What could you say about yourself, what you create, and how it's going to impact your customers in 30 seconds or less?

Here's mine: "I write books for women, helping them create the love they deserve by helping them change their behaviours so they achieve a better outcome. Whether they're trying to get over a divorce or break up, looking for the right partner, or in a relationship and wanting to make it work, I give them the tools and perspective they need to become emotional leaders and teach their partners how to have a functional and loving relationship that's free from fights."

Boom. Nice and tidy, telling the listener what I do and how my work affects others in 22.15 seconds.

There's a saying you should keep in mind all throughout this journey: Success happens when preparation meets opportunity. I'm focussed on making my product, my platform, and my presence pop with readiness almost all the time, because I never know who will cross my path, or when. If I miss an opportunity to knock the socks off someone who could have a massive impact on my forward momentum, who knows when that chance would present itself again?

The thing is, it's hard to get someone to believe in you if you're not clear about yourself. A quote I love says, "If you can't explain it simply, you don't understand it well enough." If someone asked me what I do and I went off on a long, rambling diatribe about interests and projects and current events leading into hopeful futures, the person standing in front of me would probably start checking their watch and looking around, hoping for someone to rescue them from this conversation.

We are living in a minute world. Minute meals, minute phone calls – actually, let's not even fool ourselves, we text instead of call because it takes less time – and statistics that are counted in fractions of seconds. People are in a rush to consume every moment and seemingly in a race to win at life. So if you can't explain what you do before their eyes glaze over, you're losing a potential customer every time.

It can take time to figure out what you're all about, and that's okay. Few of us come into this world with a crystal clear idea from the get go. Usually, like the human beings we are, we enter as a work in progress and iron out the kinks as we go along. And hey, maybe you're like me and start in the middle, working out details both forward and backwards when you jump into all this.

When I first started my business I went from hosting a series of workshops to condensing them into one seminar, which I then turned into my first book. From there six more books spilled out, and I figured out I love being a writer for women. But though my business model has evolved over the years, my elevator pitch has largely remained the same. I worked hard at clarifying myself in the early stages, and I have to admit being able to nail my elevator pitch also helped me understand my trajectory.

Once you've established your short business script it's time to start selling yourself anywhere and everywhere. This is where the next step comes in: becoming the best public relations representative you've ever met.

See, the number one rule of sales is to believe in the product. Passion and sincerity are huge driving factors when it comes to influence, and people want to buy something that excites them. And frankly, who is going to be more passionate about your product than you? Especially in the early stages, when few people even know what you're selling.

Becoming a PR rep means many things. Knowing the product inside and out and understanding why it's important to the client ("My photography skills center around helping women understand just how feminine and beautiful they actually are!") will only get you so far. Do you have the guts to pick up the phone and cold call places that can advance your business, so you can deliver the message you worked so hard to clarify?

Great PR reps are fearless go-getters who behave like a dog with a bone. They pinpoint where the product needs to be placed, find the people who can open those doors, and never take no from someone who isn't authorized to give it to them in the first place.

Maybe what I described isn't you, which is why you'll need to remember another golden tidbit of ageless advice: Fake it till you make it.

Now, the key to faking it effectively is being prepared. If you call up a place and fumble through your pitch they'll see right through your façade and deep into the heart of your issue – lack of confidence and knowledge.

You want to have your elevator pitch down pat, which means practicing it where it doesn't count. On friends, family, and every stranger you come across is a start. Become polished in your delivery, and your confidence in the product will shine through.

And again, never take no from someone who isn't authorized to give it. Which means before you pitch make sure you're talking to the right person.

When I wanted to set up my first book tour I called every bookstore and asked for the person in charge of scheduling in-store events. Usually they weren't available at the time or were in but wanted more information, at which point I had an email that was basically my elevator pitch, but written out and accompanied by photos. Visual appeal makes a huge difference between a yes and a no, and part of my plan was making it easy for them to say yes.

I kept a list of who I spoke to and when and what had transpired, and if I didn't hear back by the next week I called and asked for that person again. Never be afraid to be annoying, because it's tenacity that'll get you through the tougher doors!

When you're presenting yourself be sure to dress to impress. Remember to dress for the part you want, so make your look match the environment you strive to end up in. That means your promo photos are essentially forward looking statements, in essence letting your target audience imagine you in the position you want to fill.

Because as we all know, if they can conceive it, you can achieve it.

Know what your audience or the people opening doors will want from you, and fulfill that. Again, it's all about making those yes's easy to get.

As an author asking for floor space in Canada's biggest chain book seller, it was up to me find out what they'd want to see before laying out a welcome mat. So with some research my vocabulary grew to include the words "author platform." A website and social media platform like Twitter and Instagram are a must in my industry, and I made sure both were up and running before even approaching bookstores.

And because there was no reason to say no, the yes's rolled right on in.

Exercise: Make a list of where your product will fill a need. Then set a timeline for contacting those places.

_____

_____

_____

_____

_____

_____

_____

_____

Journal: Write about a time where you didn't give up and finally got what you wanted. What were you looking for? How did you get it? How did you feel when you got that "yes"?

_____

_____

_____

_____

_____

_____

_____

_____

_____

_____

Chapter 28

Set Clear Goals

If you want to be successful sooner rather than later, you'll want to be structured about your workflow. That means setting short, medium, and long term goals.

For me, this equates to writing 2,000 words a day (short), having my manuscript ready for my editing deadline (medium), and writing two books a year (long). Having clear goals that range from easy(ish) to more difficult gives a multitude of opportunities to celebrate wins, all of which are important contributors to the amount of steam you'll generate for forward momentum.

Whatever your business is, there are things you should be doing every day to help advance it. Things that will help you be plugged in for the long haul, like eating well and getting fresh air so your mental health doesn't decline. And things that give results you accumulate over time, stacking up to create that bigger success you're looking for.

So study your role models, find out what they do day to day, and start being more like them so one day you can count your chickens like they do.

Exercise: List your short, medium, and long term goals.

_____

_____

_____

_____

_____

_____

Journal: Write about something that took a long time to achieve. Break it down into what you did that fell under short term goals, medium term goals, and long term goals. Write about how you felt when you hit your final destination.

Chapter 29

Rejection Schmejection

When it comes to business, you've got to roll with the punches.

There will be doors that never open or open doors that shut. Opportunities laid out before you, then snatched back before they materialize. All this is par for the course, and you've got to be good at letting go.

I don't mean sit back and say, "Well, what will be, will be." No, I mean work your ass off and let nothing, not even twenty no's in a row, slow your roll.

Will you experience disappointment? Yes! But the depth will depend on you. If you see each no as just another stepping stone on your journey, you'll bounce back faster. But if you anticipate any particular opportunity as a make or break moment, you're setting yourself up for an emotional decline if it doesn't pan out.

Your focus needs to be more on your efforts than your outcome, because that's really the only thing you can control. What a media outlet or retail store decides is good for them isn't though, and you've got to be okay with that from the get go. Minds can change, but if you haven't been plugging away in the meantime, you won't be the one to benefit from that change when it happens.

Releasing outcomes is a way to surf above everything while you work at creating a dream career from your talent and purpose. It takes a huge amount of emotional strength to build anything from the ground up, and the one factor that eliminates 99% of the competition is an ability to handle rejection.

Personalizing rejection will absolutely tear you down, bit by bit. Taking each no to heart, allowing it to take a chunk out of your confidence and belief, will erode your desire to work hard, and you'll lose steam until you're left with zero desire to manifest your gift. So shake it off, my friend.

Meditation helps a lot, because it reduces your ability to feel fear and anxiety. That means you'll feel a blip of negative emotions when you hit a no but bounce right back because your brain isn't residing in those feelings.

Having a list of short term goals means you're not going to sit in that no. Instead, you'll just get right back to work, pounding away towards your next request and potential yes.

Maintaining perspective will help you tremendously, so keep in mind the path to the biggest yes's are paved with a ton of no's. And remember, no is never permanent. Sure, my mom said I wasn't allowed to eat the chocolate chips in the cupboard, but today I get to eat all the chocolate I want. Nothing in this life stays in a state of permanence, and that goes for those no's, too. Chances are if you stick around long enough and grow into the industry you're trying to break into, you'll hit that yes you need.

But that'll never happen if each no hits you like a punch in the gut.

So if a particular no is having a big impact on you, then it's time to make sure you're plugged in before there's a total meltdown. Practice some self-care to get yourself back on track, then hit the ground running again. Because the only outcome you'll control is whether or not you give up.

Exercise: List your three traits that make you powerful enough to withstand a thousand no's.

_____

_____

_____

_____

_____

Journal: Write a fictional story about how you got a lot of no's about your business, but then got the yes you wanted. What did that yes look like? How did you celebrate it after?

_____

_____

_____

_____

_____

_____

_____

_____

Everything
is a
lesson.

Step 5 – Discovery

The best conversations are those that lead to higher learning.

Chapter 30

Focus On Quality

You know what they say, practice makes perfect! And if there's one train of thought that keeps you forging ahead, it's the notion that you've still got room for improvement.

Now when it comes to jumping in and starting something, there's no time like the present. (Sorry, these two old clichés in a row were too appropriate to pass up.)

Which is why I highly encourage you to start everything today. I don't care if you've never made a website before, get someone to put one together then get in there and start figuring it out. I don't care if you've never written a book before, open up your computer and start typing a title, subtitle, and first paragraph. I don't care if you've never sent a Tweet before, sign up on Twitter and whip out your first Tweet with the hashtag #CauseChantalToldMeTo.

The time to start is now, and so is the time to start improving. The fact is you've gotta get step one done before you can become better. So, start. Make a list of what you need to get your purpose in front of your target audience and start chipping away at it today, beginning with what's easiest and interspersing your efforts with the harder stuff.

Cause once you've stepped into the arena you can then start honing your skills.

Look, I didn't get good at branding and creating promotional material without bombing at my first attempts. And my writing skills improved over time too, meaning the fourth edition of my first book is way better than the first edition.

You will become savvier over time, but only if you start regardless of your level of expertise. Forget waiting until you know enough to be better than you are today! You'll build your confidence, not to mention advance your evolution, by working it out as you go along.

By the way, you'll see evidence of this in my early You Tube videos. I didn't wait for my braces to come off before diving in and warming up my teaching skills. Nope. I hired myself a videographer and started making videos so I could watch myself and learn from my mistakes. Then make better videos going forward.

I didn't know anything about Instagram algorithms or hashtags, or what makes people popular on social media, but I knew fans would want a way to better understand who I was. So I opened my account anyway, playing away until I got better at sharing my life.

School is never out, Dear Reader. Not if you're the smartest student in the class. Because the ones who get ahead year after year are the ones who are always learning, improving, and displaying their evolution for all to see.

Exercise: List what you will start doing this week, this month, and this year to advance your business.

_____

_____

_____

_____

_____

Journal: Write about a time where you started something from scratch, then became good at it. What was it? How did you improve? How did you feel when someone recognized how far you'd come?

_____

_____

_____

_____

_____

_____

_____

_____

_____

_____

_____

_____

_____

_____

Chapter 31

Don't Stress About Getting What You Want

I've got to point this out because if I'm going through it, chances are you are (or will) too. In many ways we're all cut from the same cloth, you know.

I tend to stress when I get what I want. It's a weird phenomenon, but the truth isn't always pretty, is it? And I'm not the only one. Studies have found that people actually leave paid vacation days on the table year after year, then stress about wanting more vacation time.

There's something about having what we want that sometimes gives us a dose of cognitive dissonance. In other words, opposing thoughts happening inside our heads simultaneously. In this case, "I want this, it will make me feel better / I'm uncomfortable with this, and I feel anxious."

I'll want more me time, and because the Universe will pick up on that signal my media requests will slow down. Next thing you know, I'm stressing that I'm not getting more media requests.

I'll want more success, then feel overwhelmed when it comes about.

I don't know why we're so filled with push and pull emotions, but trying hard to untangle them while ignoring easy coping mechanisms won't help. So each time negative feelings pop up I get down on my knees and check under the desk to make sure I'm still plugged in.

I'll sit down with my headphones, tap into my favourite meditation track, and *Yes Goodness, thank you* my way through it. Because frankly, I'm an idiot if I allow myself to feel bad by stressing over what I've been asking for.

Exercise: List situations where you realize you had cognitive dissonance and felt uncomfortable getting what you wanted.

_____

_____

_____

_____

_____

Journal: Write a short story in which you'll receive something amazing that you really want and describe how you'll wholeheartedly accept it.

_____

_____

_____

_____

_____

_____

_____

_____

_____

Chapter 32

Pick Your Crowd Like a Pro

Nothing makes learning easier than following in footsteps. Let me bring you back to that Everest analogy again. Don't you think it's easier to place your boot inside the step created already by the person walking in front of you instead of trying to break through a layer of ice and snow to create your own indentation? Don't you think it's easier to walk the trail that's already established instead of trying to create a new one and potentially falling off a treacherous rocky face?

There's nothing wrong with walking the same path great achievers have forged for us already. In fact, it's the smart thing to do. Those Sherpas leading you up the mountain know the safest way to bring you back alive is to keep to the path of familiarity, because they already know it's the best route.

Look, I'm not telling you to be a cookie cutter in your purpose and business. Your uniqueness lies is your talent, your personal branding, you personality, and your approach when you work with your target audience. But when it comes to marketing and business there are tried and true methods that shouldn't be ignored.

And we're sponges by nature. Mother Nature wanted to make sure we had the best chances of survival when we lived among the plants and animals, so she ingrained us with a desire to watch, learn, and imitate others in order to shorten our learning curve. The faster we picked up on what was safe versus dangerous, the better chance we had of not succumbing to Darwin's Theory of evolution – the smartest survive while the dumbest fail to learn from others' mistakes and successes.

That's why it's important to pay attention to who you're surrounding yourself with. Because typically you'll follow the crowd, and if your crowd keeps painting itself into a corner, you unwittingly increase your odds of finding yourself in a similar situation.

But choosing your closest comrades from among the savviest and wisest, even if they're people you'll never meet but admire for being where you want to be, will help you plan your work schedule and business more successfully.

Exercise: Make a list of 3 character traits you most admire in people.

_____

_____

_____

_____

_____

_____

_____

Journal: Write about what steps you'll take to better emulate those traits.

_____

_____

_____

I am not afraid to imagine my greatness.

Step 6 – Intimacy

Successful people are masters in manifestation.

Chapter 33

Become One With Your Vision

"Money is an energy! Become a money magnet! Clear your blocks!"

There are a lot of spiritual business gurus who will chant this over and over, hypnotizing you with the notion that if you can dream up buckets of cash, they'll eventually pour from the sky. And they're not far off.

The message they're extolling is one of manifestation, something we shouldn't ignore in all this. There are numerous super successful people who say they pictured themselves arriving at their final destination all along, never giving up on the picture inside their brains on what "making it" looked like.

For Jim Carrey it was a 10 million dollar cheque. For Sylvester Stallone it was starring in the screenplay he wrote. For Arnold Schwarzenegger it was walking off a stage with a Mr. Universe title. All of these people used a powerful strategy in conjunction with their physical efforts: the power of their imagination.

But it wasn't only their imagination they empowered. They infected everyone around them with the picture inside their heads, exuding it through their pores in every way possible. Their words were full of confidence in their journey, and from the clothing they wore to the swagger in their walks they showed the world they were already there, and simply waiting for everyone else to catch up.

Manifestation is such an important part of your business because that forward thinking energy helps put opportunities in your path.

Did that just sound weird? Well then, welcome to a world where not everything can be explained in ways that we're used to.

It's not easy to put the intangible into words. But when you can bring forth real life experiences to help define the undefinable, it gets a little easier. Jim Carrey got his 10 million dollar cheque on the date he said he would. Sylvester Stallone got that leading role, and Arnold won his Mr. Universe title.

The thing is, you can do everything except imagine the success you want, and roll the dice about gaining something you're not even spending time picturing in your mind.

Or.

You can become intimate with your deepest dreams, really bring them into the light, and clearly see yourself basking in the payoff your sustained efforts will bring you.

Which scenario sounds best?

Yeah, I thought so.

I bring this up under the Intimacy umbrella because you really do need to become intricately entangled with your business. And not only what it is right now, but what it could become under your care. Just like any relationship, as long as you choose the type that's right for you you'll get out what you put in. So it does take some care, attention to detail, and a belief that the future will unfold in amazing ways.

Imagination has always been something that kept us on the right path. When cavemen could imagine danger lurking in dark caves they tread cautiously. And when they could imagine more plentiful food on the horizon they ate to live another day.

Imagination is a tool to be used wisely. It's a curse if you dwell on negatives and allow yourself to be pulled so far from your dreams you completely lose sight of them. Or it's a motivator that gets you up in the morning to pound out another hour of work. When used right, manifesting is a symptom of believing in yourself.

I started my business talking about the intricacies of relationships and what makes them either incredibly magical or colossal failures. Throughout my books I drop a lot of what I call Chantal'isms, one of them a comparison of components for a relationship to parts of a bicycle. "If love was a bicycle, faith would be one of the wheels," I said.

Think about that. What's a bike without a wheel? A cumbersome piece of machinery that isn't going to get you somewhere anytime soon.

You need faith in yourself as you travel this (maybe) long, sometimes hard road. But how will that faith take form? It starts inside your mind, created in the picture you can see for yourself when everything you've wanted comes to fruition.

So be bold and be the best there ever was when you picture your future self. You never know how many pieces of that puzzle will actually fall into place.

Exercise: Regularly use some of your meditation minutes to imagine your ultimate outcome. Use the journaling exercise below to inspire your thoughts.

_____

_____

_____

_____

_____

_____

Journal: Describe your absolute highest goal in a scene. Where are you? What is happening? How are you feeling? Make this as vivid as possible!

_____

_____

_____

_____

_____

_____

_____

Chapter 34

Stage Your Home

I don't know about you, but I'm a junkie for reality shows that follow high powered real estate agents. What can I say, I follow my own advice and fill my sights with the best of the best, hoping some of their smarts will rub off on me!

Anyway, I find there's an important lesson to gleam from them. Staging can make or break a sale, and the more you're asking for the more influential staging is to the bottom line.

So what does staging look like for you? Well, if you're a jeweler, then great photography means your product will be seen in all its glory. If you're a public speaker, your clothing, hair, and makeup, along with great posture and confident delivery is key. If you make skin care your branding and bottles will help tell the story about how natural the ingredients are.

In essence, staging is the visual message people pick up right away. And like staging a home on the market, it helps the client understand whether or not what they're seeing is the right fit. Is this worth buying into or not? Does this accommodate me? Will this fit my needs? Does this instill trust in me? Does this product excite me?

Staging yourself or your products needs to happen in such a way that full communication happens on first sight. Look, never underestimate just how lazy people actually are. Marketing 101 starts with teaching that 1) the less clicks it takes to gain access to a purchase page, the less buyers you'll lose along the way, and 2) the less independent research someone feels they need to make, the more likely you are to keep their attention.

For the most part, people don't want to spend too much time figuring stuff out. So if you can convey a ton of understanding in a minimal amount of time, you're more likely to create a client.

Don't assume people will understand how sparkly your jewellery is; show it. Don't assume people will wait around long enough to understand how competent you are; show it. Don't assume they'll buy your skin care products because you say they're natural and organic and the total bomb. Show it.

Stage your products, stage your website, stage your appearance, and you'll close the gap between what you offer and someone's understanding of it.

Exercise: Define what it means to stage your particular product.

_____

_____

_____

_____

_____

_____

Journal: Describe a time where visual appeal was influential in your purchasing decision. What stood out? How did it make you feel?

_____

_____

Chapter 35

Great Power Requires Great Control

I have those very words on one of my vision boards, reminding me that this journey isn't always easy. But those hard moments are just that, moments, and with a little discipline I can forge through them and gain a little more towards my goals.

Intimacy isn't always a path of rainbow farting glitter covered unicorns. In couples, the path to intimacy is littered with sorted out communications and realizations about shared ideals. It's a growing sensation that you're forming a team, one that will work together through good times and bad, so you can both realize the shared goal of having your ride or die till the very end.

Intimacy is at its core the product of a journey.

One that requires self-control, introspection, and accountability for your actions. It requires honesty, focus, sacrifice, and an ability to put in the work anytime, anywhere. It takes openness and vulnerability, a willingness to allow yourself and your emotions to be stripped bare, then rebuilt all over again to include more in your life.

But you have to be willing to do all that so you and your purpose driven business can come together. Otherwise, you'll watch your dreams fall by the side of the road, then wither and die from thirst and starvation.

So you've got two choices. Feed your dreams your heart and soul, or starve your dreams till they crumble into dust. But if you got this far into this book, I think I already know which path you're choosing.

There are many work-shy, unfocussed dreamers out there. People who spew cookie cutter meme quotes all day long while slowly spinning lazy wheels of self-fulfilling prophecies. "Oh, I was going to do this, but it's too hard." They're the ones downgrading dreams to hobbies because lo and behold, they weren't up to the task of applying themselves.

Let me be a word nerd here and lay out the words that are synonymous with intimacy: closeness, confidence, affection, attachment, togetherness. Just like in any union, you want to become deeply familiar with your business so you care about growth, evolution, and how you can mature together. You want to step into your business relationship with a willingness to get through the tough moments so you can reap the rewards these efforts give you.

Exercise: List what it is about your business that complements you. In what ways do you make a great couple?

_____

_____

_____

_____

_____

Journal: Describe the ways in which developing your product is helping you become a better human being.

_____

Chapter 36

Haters Gonna Hate

"If you don't have any haters you're not that gifted." ~ Bishop Noel Jones

"Haters are fans in denial." ~ Adam Rippon

You might find yourself garnering some uncomfortable attention, especially from those who thought they'd be further along in life than they are today. They're watching with jealousy as you roar past the stagnant spot they've ended up at, and unfortunately, you might step in the vomit spewing out of them.

Sure, it sucks to have to deal with their negativity. You definitely need to develop a thick skin and lean on coping mechanisms to keep your head above the fray. But the last thing you want to do is drown in their words and actions, and in the process lose focus on your own forward momentum.

Understand that these people are like jealous ex-lovers of the success you're now enjoying. Their relationship with the road you're on crumbled due to their laziness and sense of entitlement, and a refusal to shed their ego to make it work. Now, they see their old flame snuggled up in bed with you and they can't stand it.

They stalk you online, leaving little clues behind like bunny turds in grass. They speak bitter words behind your back, telling others there's no way you deserve the recognition you're getting. They ignore the fact that they're not where you are through their own fault and turn their self-loathing outward in an attempt to escape an undeniable truth. That when it comes to creating a solid relationship with anything you've got to have work ethic, and a willingness to own your mistakes and learn from them.

I talked earlier about how people who never realize their dreams are those who feel entitled to them just for showing up. "If I build it, all will happen in my favour," they think, and so their efforts stop too soon. They don't realize marriages don't work just because they got married, and businesses don't succeed just because they put out a product. Their unwillingness to take responsibility for their actions are major contributors to the fact that they're sitting on the sidelines today, watching you soar past on your way to the finish line.

So, rather than being bothered by their smallness, it might be more appropriate to feel sorry for them. Sorry that they harass their own feelings by poking themselves in the eye every time they seek you out on social media, hoping to see you fail, only to witness your growth. Sorry that their willful ignorance will continuously block their path at every turn. Sorry that they'll find themselves leaving dreams behind because they just don't want to deal with the work and sacrifice.

I know it'll likely bother you if someone has a negative reaction to your growth. But it's up to you to choose your next emotional destination. And this here is the core of all my lessons: you can choose to either stay in the flush of your ego and swim in denial and pointed fingers, or you can choose to use your mind to pull you closer to reality where real life success happens through your conscious efforts.

When people spew unprovoked negativity in your direction it's not about you. It's about their own inner turmoil combined with avoidance tactics. If they'd rather focus on how they think you're underserving instead of how they can achieve more, that's their life path to deal with.

So go ahead. Shake it off. Do an extra ten minutes of meditation to counterbalance the reaction you had. Go for a walk to move your mind forward. Vent to a friend (But never react to the drama directly! It only feeds the beast). And re-read this chapter to remind yourself of the perspective you need.

Not everyone chooses to develop intimacy with everything important in their lives. But *your* greatest comfort will ultimately stem from the work you put in to receive all the gifts true intimacy can give you.

Exercise: List your character traits that help you rise above the negative behaviours of others.

_____

_____

_____

_____

_____

_____

Journal: Describe a time when someone tried to pull you down and you ignored their efforts. What did they try to do? How did you rise above it? How did you feel at the end of it all?

_____

_____

_____

_____

_____

_____

_____

_____

_____

_____

_____

_____

_____

Give it away
till they can't
live without it.

Step 7 – Love

There is no greater verb than this one – to love.

Chapter 37

Hustle From the Heart

There's a difference between *doing something* and *being on fire*. Usually when people are just going through the motions they're more into the breaks they find between tasks than the feeling of accomplishment that accompanies working hard. But when someone is on fire, stand back. Cause the flames jumpin' off them might cause a touch of heat stroke.

When you tap into your purpose it's like the whole world has shifted. When you hit that stride most of the time all you can think about is what you'll do the moment you can open your laptop (or crafting basket) again. Your mind is engulfed with creativity, drive, and purpose driven actions, and you're always ready for more. More information, more help, and more work because it just doesn't feel like work. And through it all you're actually having fun.

When I talk about relationships I tell my readers love is a verb, found in the things you do to make your partner happy. And if we look at the relationship you're developing with your purpose, that same rule applies. Will you show it the love it deserves?

Will you respect and cherish it? Will you uplift and support it? Will you give it the consideration it needs to grow? And will you lean into its needs, gladly doing what must be done to turn love into a verb, not just something you say?

Love is not an easy journey. You have to twist and turn yourself around in order to leave behind negative conditioning and become a more functional member of the team. You have to recognize then swallow your ego so it doesn't interfere with necessary actions and behaviours. You have to spend time reflecting on yourself so you can pinpoint your shortcomings and change them. And you have to become adept at practicing forgiveness, because nobody's perfect and mistakes are inevitable.

But part of the beauty of love is how it unfolds in the journey. You become better at self-love, better at calming and controlling yourself, better at choosing to do things that make you happy in the long run, versus satisfied in the moment. And best of all, you infect those around you with an inspiring new way of being.

But if you're not hustling from the heart, if you're not putting in all this time and effort for the pure joy of seeing results accumulate one on top of the other, you're not really in love. And if you're not filling your purpose with true love before unleashing it, it risks coming across in lackluster ways.

Exercise: Rate your love for your product on a scale of 1 – 10.

_____

_____

_____

_____

Journal: Describe the ways in which you'll fill your product with even more love.

_____

_____

_____

Chapter 38

Light Up Every Room

Two of my three vision boards have these words: I will light up every room I walk into.

It's important to carry your intent and purpose with you everywhere you go. Offering your talent is only a part of the equation; you need to *be* the light you want to create. Maybe you make jewellery designed to help women feel beautiful and feminine, which means every time you enter a room you want people to pick up on the vibe that your purpose is beauty and femininity. Maybe you make organic, cruelty-free skin care, and the light you infuse every room with is one of planetary care and compassion accompanying your glowing, radiant skin. Maybe your yoga program centers around

PTSD healing, and so the intent you'll light every room with is one of calm, caring understanding.

The bottom line is, you need to be the essence of your product. Only then will you be believable, and only then will people trust you and what you offer.

Take a moment for a deep breath and align yourself with your vision before walking into a room. Do what you need to protect your energy from unexpected drama and uncontrollable situations. Keep you game face on at all times by making sure you're shrinking your amygdala during calm days so you're better adapted for dealing with stressful ones.

If you allow your light to be frequently dimmed, if you allow people and circumstances to interfere with your energy, if you're not in control of yourself and what you project, then your messaging will be skewed. The result? You might become increasingly jaded until this ride has lost all of its fun and you just want to get off before you puke.

A good way to maintain your glow is to be thankful for all things at all times. That might have just sounded a little unrealistic, but if you can tap into this philosophy each time you feel yourself waning, you'll find a really useful tool. Gratitude is a great mind shifter and a huge light source of personal energy. It's a vibe that feels like love because it truly *is* love. And the fact is, regardless of the situation, there's something good to be found. The onus is on you to search far enough to pinpoint it, and make that your focus.

And the Universe, like any sweet souled lover, never lets a feeling of gratitude go unrewarded.

Exercise: List 3 reasons people can trust you and your product.

_____

_____

_____

_____

_____

Journal: Describe what makes you grateful about the product you're creating. What has it brought to your life? What about it absolutely warms your heart?

_____

_____

_____

Chapter 39

Give It Away Till They Can't Live Without It

If you want people to buy your books, write plenty of blog posts and create videos showing you know what you're talking about. If you want people to buy your skin care, give away samples so they understand how different your product feels on their face. Be so passionate about your product you're shouting it from the rooftops at every opportunity and letting people sample its effects at every turn.

Word of mouth is bar none the most effective advertising tool at your disposal. I actually conducted a short survey at the last fundraiser I helped organize, and almost every attendee said they came because a friend asked them to. And many people will look up

Amazon reviews even before buying a product in a brick and mortar store, just to get an idea of other people's impression first.

This philosophy of giving away your product at every turn has a ton of benefits. It helps you practice practice practice, giving you opportunities to hone your skills. It gives people a taste of what you're all about, and if that taste ends up being yummy, they'll become your walking billboards, extolling the virtues of who you are and what you can do everywhere they go.

It's just that there's no selfishness in real love. I'm always giving away my advice (and sometimes even books!) because I thrive on the love that's created when people follow my steps. If your greatest reward isn't found in the simple act of giving, then it's not true love.

I'm happy for all the time I spent giving everything I had every time I could. It's that effort that got me splashed across Lifestyle pages throughout Canada and continues to sell my books on Amazon.

When I speak to women dealing with the dating scene I teach them that there are two types of people out there. Selfish, short term thinkers are the type not suited for long term love. But generous, long term thinkers are exactly the sort of person you can create a beautiful lifelong relationship with.

Which type are you? Make no mistake, the return you get from your purpose will equal what you put into it. Short term thinking may give you short term gains, but only long term thinking combined with generosity of spirit will give you more than you imagined.

Exercise: List how you'll give your product away.

_____

_____

_____

_____

_____

Journal: Describe a moment where you had zero selfishness and felt pure joy giving something away. What was it? How did you feel giving it? What was the end result for the receiver? How did that affect you emotionally in the long run?

_____

_____

Chapter 40

Balance

Love never requires complete self-sacrifice. It recognizes the need for balance, and so should you. You can never fully give love from an empty vessel, which means you've got to make sure your love bank is topped off before you start trying to spread that good stuff all over the place.

If I hadn't learned this important lesson, I wouldn't be where I am today. My current relationship would have become divorce #2, and this business would have flopped from a lack of energy to see it through.

Plus, it's just natural to balance. And I mean that on a fundamental, the Universe wouldn't exist without balance, kind of way. For every life born on this planet there's a death, and vice versa. When food is plentiful life increases, when food is scarce the number of living beings decrease. With every inhale there is an exhale.

It's natural for you to want to forge full steam ahead with your business, and it's also natural for you to want to draw back, spend more time with friends and family, and chillax with a cold mochaccino or glass of wine.

It's natural for you to want to unplug from your computer and bask in nature for a while. It's natural for you to want to spend a few days not looking at a single email or dong a single yoga pose. It's natural to just veg for the sake of vegging, letting your brain take a vacation.

Don't deny yourself what you need to fill your soul with self-love. Understanding and practicing this early on can mean the difference between enjoying every ounce success has to offer and someone who's "made it" but ends up shackled with a drug or alcohol problem because their lack of self-love won't allow them to enjoy the fruits of their labour.

Exercise: List what you'll do to maintain balance in your life.

_____

_____

_____

_____

Journal: Finish this sentence: "I know I'm loving myself when _____."

_____

_____

_____

_____

_____

_____

_____

_____

_____

_____

_____

_____

Chapter 41

Because Love

When I wrote *Say Yes To Goodness* I deviated from my usual 7 steps. As the outline for that book spun itself out, 10 vital ways to ensure your life is on track spilled out of my mind.

The very first step in that book talks about the importance of picking a worthy partner. Someone who will not only support you, but follow you on your path towards ever increasing mental, emotional, and spiritual growth. But this step comes with a warning: worthy partners are difficult to be with, at least in the beginning.

The challenge lies in how their good qualities will magnify your shortcomings, forcing you to face what you must change in order to evolve. They'll challenge your ego, and if you don't rise above those white hot ego flashes of emotion, you'll end up spinning in the same places over and over. Because blaming others for how you're failing never gets you closer to success.

Look, as we dance our way through our individual lives, we'll take many hands, choosing partners for short or long periods of time. Some will affect us more than others, but all will have some sort of influence on how we view our past, our present, and our future selves.

What you choose to do with your time and efforts ends up being one of those partners, and that relationship can get as tricky as human to human relationships. Because if you stay too long with the wrong partner, they'll spin you in ways that make you nauseous, and it won't be long before you're tired of their clumsy feet and bad breath. "Let go already," you'll think from the moment you get out of bed until the moment your head hits the pillow again.

But what you might not realize is, you're the one holding on too tightly to the wrong set of hands.

Fear might be a reason. We tend to seek what's familiar, even if that familiarity sucks. We're afraid of what's around un-explored corners, so we keep a vicelike grip on that crappy partner, ignoring the fact that we're feeling sick and getting stepped on. Often, we fear a challenge we haven't tried to overcome yet. Like letting go.

Steve Harvey often says, "You've just gotta jump." You don't know what's on the other side, but you sure as hell know what you're already experiencing. Sometimes you just need to take a deep breath, hope for the best, and leap into your next evolution.

But it needs to be worthy, and you need to be prepared to be challenged.

Starting any new relationship is hard, and beginning a relationship with your purpose and turning it into a business won't be easy. There will be moments to celebrate, like anniversaries, new rollouts, and increasing recognition for your hard work. But there will be times where you'll cry and wish you had the strength to break up and walk away once and for all, because you're buckling under the pressure change always puts us under.

Because before it gets easy, it's bound to get hard.

Having a magical relationship with my husband came after years of hardship. I had to reformulate my brain from top to bottom, tossing out old ways of thinking and reassessing the world I lived in. I had to change my behaviours, the words coming out of my mouth, and even my emotions.

But I persevered, and I earned an incredible life with an incredible man.

Having a business that changes lives came with years of hardship too. I had to deal with costly mistakes, people who didn't follow through, and opportunities that teased themselves into view, only to fade off before becoming real. Not to mention my sore ass from sitting and writing so many books in a short period of time.

Every love in your life will come at a cost. But if you're not choosing something worthy, the cost ends up being lost time, eroded self-esteem, and ever increasing frustration with the direction your life is going. But choosing something (or someone) worthy to love will cost you old, dysfunctional habits, and mindsets that keep you from growing into your best version.

So choose wisely, my friend. Make everything you bring into your life worthy of your efforts, and you'll rise beyond anything you could have imagined.

Exercise: Pay it forward! Go on Amazon and leave a review about this book. Write your first draft here.

_____

_____

_____

_____

_____

Journal: Write about the fresh thoughts that make you feel more motivated now than before. What has changed in your mind? What makes you feel more inspired? How will you use that inspiration to inspire others?

_____

_____

_____

_____

_____

_____

_____

Afterword

We are all custom made.

Custom made to create. Custom made to love. Custom made to feel, explore, and learn. The mechanisms of our brains and bodies never cease to fascinate me, and though I've been studying *us* for decades, I know I'm only scratching the surface.

It's unfortunate that we've often struggled with a push/pull that's entwined in our culture. "Figure out what you'll do when you're done with school!" said the counsellors in Grade 9 as they sat me in front of tests designed to help me find my life's path. Zoologist is what came up for me. I guess they didn't take into account my mad typing skills.

"You've got to get your grades up!" they said at the same time, forcing me to put aside the novel I was engrossed in so I could memorize what year the Northwest Passage was discovered.

And you know what? I almost had children because *that's what society said I should do* once I had the husband, car, and salaried career promising a sweet pension package. I'm thankful my first husband had cold feet at the time, because once I took a year to think about it I realized maybe I was better off being a fur mamma.

It takes a lot of courage to swim against societal tides and forge your own way, regardless of those who think they know what you should be doing. If you don't learn to speak the truth when your heart points you in a particular direction, you end up living a standard life, all the while trying to define what makes you *uniquely* you.

And when I look at the lasting, sometimes damaging effects those pushes and pulls have on our emotions, our relationships, and our general happiness in life, I can't help but wonder, what if?

What if everyone was born into a world that automatically supported their needs, regardless of demographic? What if, from day one, everyone was free to explore their depths, to choose their own path, and to fall into whatever pulled them with the most strength?

What if nobody had to suffer fear, pain, hunger, or crisis? What if nobody had to "pay the bills", trudging their way through jobs as they counted the hours till they could close their eyes, pretending they weren't sleepwalking already.

What if moms could be moms, surrounded by other moms who'd been moms and were eager to help new moms become awesome moms? Instead of stoically doing too much on their own because someone told them that this was the new "powerful"?

What if boys were supported in all their natural glory, and were uplifted, strengthened, and shown that being emotional was as natural as breathing? Instead of being stifled and misled about "real" masculinity, leaving them untrained and unprepared for intimate, lasting love?

What if we had a world where our fearful, anxious brains were all calmed, and each and every person on this planet spent daily time in silence, doing nothing but appreciating their existence and the support they get from others? Instead of walking around vomiting fear and ego in every direction, creating a ripple of victims and perpetrators in our wake?

What a wonderful world that would be, indeed.

I know this will never happen in my lifetime. But I believe in collective consciousness, I believe in the power of infection, I believe in epigenetics and our ability to genetically transmit happiness, and I believe in you, my fellow human.

I already know you have the ability to calm your mind, spread your love, and create something that will resonate for generations. I also know that we are monkeys, designed to learn through imitation, which means I know your children will learn the Goodness you're creating and spread that down to their little ones too. And I believe, in this way, that we can change the world.

Are you with me?

Yeah, you are. So welcome my friend, to this journey of awesomeness. To a revolution of the soul. To an uplift that resonates clear as a bell, down through generations as they take the hope and skills we've developed and run with them.

Welcome to a world we may never see, but will influence nonetheless. So Namaste, my brothers and sisters. The light in me recognizes the light in you.

About The Author

CHANTAL LIVES IN ONTARIO, Canada, with her husband Dennis and two dogs, Maggie and Lulu. She is a Human Relations and behavioural expert with a successful practice, helping clients learn how to find and keep a "magical" loving relationship. As a public speaker, workshop leader, private coach, writer, and frequent media contributor, Chantal is busy distributing advice far and wide in the hopes of creating loving unions that will resonate for generations. Chantal is also a member of Zonta, a UN recognized international organization of professional women working together to advance the status of women worldwide through service and advocacy.

Visit Chantal Heide at

www.CanadasDatingCoach.com

You Tube – Chantal Heide

Instagram – @canadasdatingcoach

Twitter – @CanDatingCoach

Facebook – Chantal Heide, Canada's Dating Coach

Itunes – Chantal Heide

Pinterest – Canada's Dating Coach